Cash is *Still* King

Keith Checkley

Apart from any fair dealing for the purpose of research or private study, or criticism or review, as permitted under the Copyright, Designs and Patents Act 1988, this publication may be reproduced, stored or transmitted, in any form or by any means, only with the prior permission in writing of the publisher, or in the case of reprographic reproduction in accordance with the terms and licenses issued by the Copyright Licensing Agency. Enquiries concerning the reproduction outside those terms should be addressed to the publishers at the following address:

> The Chartered Institute of Bankers
> Emmanuel House
> 4-9 Burgate Lane
> Canterbury
> Kent
> CT1 2XJ
> United Kingdom

Chartered Institute of Bankers Publications are published by The Chartered Institute of Bankers, a non-profit making registered educational charity and are distributed exclusively by Bankers Books which is a wholly owned subsidiary of The Chartered Institute of Bankers.

The Chartered Institute of Bankers, the authors and all contributors believe that the sources of information on which this book is based are reliable and has made every effort to ensure the complete accuracy of the text. However, neither The Chartered Institute of Bankers, the authors nor any contributor can accept any legal responsibility whatsoever for consequences that may arise from any errors or omissions or any opinion or advice given.

Typesetting: Kevin O'Connor
Printer: Creative Print and Design

Copyright © Keith Checkley 1999

ISBN 0-85297 474 4

Contents

Introduction	v
Acknowledgements	viii
Chapter 1 - Cash Flow and Business	1
Chapter 2 - Case Study: ERF	30
Chapter 3 - Cash Flow and the Bank	72
Chapter 4 - Cash Flow and the Bank: Illustrative Case Studies	106
Chapter 5 - Cash Flow and Restructuring	136
Chapter 6 - Case Study: The Canadian Aluminium Company	158
Chapter 7 - Case Study: Sime Darby	184
Bibliography	196
Index	198

DEDICATION

To Ella – a determined little lady

INTRODUCTION

In 1994, Financial Times/Pitman Publishing completed the publication of my book *Cash is King – A Practical Guide to Strategic Cash Management*. In it, I explained that the strategic management of cash flow is essential to survival of any business, be it large or small. Cash is the fuel to drive the business – without it, the business will certainly fail. I am pleased to now have the opportunity to revisit this important topic. In response to requests, in this new book I have included a little less tutorial text and more case study illustration.

I would like to be able to tell you that, in the modern global market place, cash handling and usage has improved; but the reporting of financial results within stock market quoted companies continues to emphasize simple yardsticks, such as P/E ratios, with little emphasis on the companies' cash-generating abilities. We have also seen tremendous volatility – particularly recently in the Far East. Not only in general commercial business, but also in banks, many of which in Thailand, Indonesia, Malaysia, China and even Japan have come under liquidity management pressures.

> **Japan Admits Full Scale of Banks' Bad Debts** - *Financial Times* 28/7/95
>
> Mr. Sei Nakai, Deputy Director General of the Ministry's Banking Bureau, told foreign financial analysts at an unprecedented briefing that the banking system's bad loans stood at almost ¥58,000 bn (£335 bn), equivalent to more than a tenth of the entire Japanese economy.

> **Problem Loans Trail World Bank** - *Financial Times* 25/9/95
>
> The World Bank has stepped up its efforts to improve supervision of its loan projects, but the number of 'problem' projects is still climbing.

Asia Turmoil - *Business News* 14/11/97

China has significant bank difficulties with almost 20% of all loans in the problem loan category. IMF and World Bank in proposed $1.3 bn package to restructure Thai financial markets - bad loans of around $35.8 bn estimated. On November 1st, the Government closed 16 Indonesian Banks saying that they were unhealthy and insolvent.

As I write today in 1999, even countries cannot ignore our topic:

More Pain and No Gain as Asian Economies Fight On - *Financial Times* 1/8/98

Japan's unemployment rate soared to a record level and the yen tumbled as the Asian crisis deepened and a credit agency warned that £60 bn was needed to stave off bank collapses. China's central bank stepped in to defend its currency, and in Korea, car giant Hyundai sparked fears of a long strike by sacking 1,500 workers.

Credit Agency Fitch IBCA puts the cost of rescuing Indonesia's banks at up to 35% of its national output. In Korea and Thailand, the figure is 20% to 25%.

West Fears Snub as Russia Shuffles Pack - *Financial Times* 24/8/98

Foreign bankers in Moscow were anxious as officials prepared to unveil the terms of the country's debt rescheduling, after Russia said a week ago that it was to default on its short-term rouble denominated debt.

The debt announcement was due last week, but was deferred until today amid hopes that the terms would be made more favourable to Western lenders. Russia needed to reschedule the debt to break the crippling cycle of having to find *cash* each week to repay short-term loans, and having to borrow the money by issuing more short-term paper at yields above 100%.

To conclude this introduction, I therefore have no hesitation in stating that Cash is **still** King and that each and every type of business must continue to strive to improve its strategic cash management techniques.

ACKNOWLEDGEMENTS

I am particularly grateful to Eric Dobby and Philip Blake of The Chartered Institute of Bankers for their commissioning of this project and to Claire for her patience in editing and formatting my script; also to Keith Dickinson FCIB for once again contributing to the written contents of the book. Finally to Marcus Nidd for case study assistance and Beverley of the CIB Research Unit.

Keith Checkley
January 1999

1
CASH FLOW AND BUSINESS

Cash flows are normally reported in a *Cash Flow Statement*. In the United Kingdom this is prepared in accordance with Financial Reporting Standard (FRS) No. 1 - Cash Flow Statements. In countries that have adopted international accounting standards it is prepared in accordance with International Accounting Standard (IAS) No. 7 - Cash flow Statements. The Cash Flow Statement is a relatively recent phenomenon. FRS 1 was issued in the United Kingdom in September 1991. IAS 7, having originally been called Statement of Changes in Financial Position, was revised in 1992 and retitled Cash Flow Statements. Prior to this the UK and many other countries required a Statement of Source and Application of Funds in the annual accounts which, while being a document that assisted in the analysis of cash flows, was *not* a cash flow statement and proved difficult to interpret.

Ever since the joint stock company was invented in the 1800s it has been customary to offer shareholders an annual Profit and Loss Account and Balance Sheet. However, professional analysts have realized that cash flows are essentially a matter of fact and are therefore much less prone to accounting interpretation by managers and directors of companies. Consequently we are now seeing much more emphasis being placed on the identification and analysis of cash flows as opposed to the traditional approach of data derived from the Profit and Loss Account and Balance Sheet

See overleaf for extract from FRS 1 - Illustrative example

XYZ LIMITED
Cash flow statement for the year ended 31 March 1992

	£'000	£'000
Net cash inflow from operating activities		
(see note below)		6889
Return on investments and servicing of finance		
Interest received	3011	
Interest paid	(12)	
Dividends paid	(2417)	
Net cash inflow from returns on investment		
and servicing of finance		582
Taxation		
Corporation tax paid (including advance		
corporation tax)	(2922)	
Tax paid		(2922)
Investing activities		
Payments to acquire intangible fixed assets	(71)	
Payments to acquire tangible fixed assets	(1496)	
Receipts from sales of tangible fixed assets	42	
Net cash outflow from investing activities		(1525)
Net cash inflow before financing		3024
Financing		
Issue of ordinary share capital	211	
Repurchase of debenture loans	(149)	
Expenses paid in connection with share issues	(5)	
Net cash inflow from financing		57
Increase in cash and cash equivalents		3081

Note to the cash flow statement
Reconciliation of operating profit to net cash inflow from operating activities:

	£'000
Operating profit	6022
Depreciation charges	893
Loss on sale of tangible fixed assets	6
Increase in stocks	(194)
Increase in debtors	(72)
Increase in creditors	234
	6889

1. **Net cash inflow from operating activities**

   The identification starts with operating profit, and the next two items are depreciation and the (profit)/loss on sale of fixed assets, which are added back. The objective is to identify the *cash generated from operations*. This is normally achieved by *adding back to operating profit all non-cash items* in the Profit and Loss Account before the operating profit value is struck. Additional items in this class include loss and trade provisions, unrealized gains and losses on foreign exchange and provisions in respect of acquisitions and reorganizations.

   The second three items, the increase or decrease in stocks, debtors and creditors, gives us the *movement in the investment in net working assets*. Most businesses are constantly increasing their investment in stock and debtors to allow for the effects of inflation and growth in turnover of the business. This is usually partly offset by the increase in creditors each year, which arises for the same reasons.

   So the *cash generated from operations* less the *amount invested in net working assets* every period gives us the **Net cash inflow from operating activities**.

2. **Returns on investments and servicing of finance**

   The cash flow statement of XYZ Limited shows interest received and the interest and dividends paid.

   Interest received is the cash earned from surplus cash. We would also find any dividends received from investments in this section, because these are earnings from investments. Where the business owns less than 50% of the shares and therefore does not enjoy control, it makes sense where these items are material to separate this cash flow item for analysis purposes. This is because the future flow of dividends from investments may be less certain than the business's own core-operating cash flow.

Indeed we also need to separate interest and dividends *paid* in order to properly evaluate the performance of the business, because these payments are driven by quite different factors:

- The payment of interest is contractual and may vary significantly depending on the inflation and interest rate outlook for the business concerned and the amount of interest which is at fixed rather then at variable rates.
- The timing and amount of dividends paid by the business, in contrast, is at the discretion of the directors.

3. **Taxation**
This item is the amount *paid* in the financial period. In the United Kingdom this represents the tax due in respect of profits earned in the previous accounting period. In other countries the grace period for payment of taxes due varies from monthly on account to nine months after the year end, as it is in the United Kingdom.

Note that there is no reference to deferred tax in the cash flow statement. This is because any charge or release for deferred tax in the Profit and Loss Account tax charge is a movement in the deferred tax *provision* and is therefore a *non-cash item. Non-cash items have no effect on the cash flow statement.*

4. **Investing activities**
This is the section where we find the value of capital expenditure made during the period under examination. The term "capital expenditure" is often abbreviated to "capex". Where it is netted off against any proceeds of disposal it is often known as "net capex". Do not confuse the *profit or loss on the sale of fixed assets* (which actually represents an adjustment to the depreciation charge) with the *proceeds of sale of fixed assets* (which represents the cash received on the sale of fixed assets). A cash flow statement shows any proceeds of sale as a cash inflow in this section.

5. **Net cash inflow before financing**
This is the key cash flow figure. Items 1 to 4 above represent the cash generation and cash absorbed in reinvestment in the fixed and working

assets of the business, paying taxes and compensating providers of finance. The cash flow generated (or cash flow absorbed) is what remains after carrying out these essential activities.

6. **Financing**

    This final section shows how the cash surplus has been used (and, if it is cash absorbed, how it has been financed). The sum of the movements on equity, debt and cash when totalled should equal the net cash inflow/(outflow) before financing.

    Presentations of the financing section vary. In this case the cash has been shown separately as the final figure. Sometimes all the movements are shown, with a total which equals the *net cash inflow before financing.*

The FRS1 document or its international equivalent will therefore provide a useful template for us to examine and monitor the essential constituent cash flow dynamics of any business, whatever its size or sector.

Cash Flow and Business Cycles

We will begin our cash flow topic by restating from my first book *Cash is King*, a diagrammatic approach to the capital cycle. (See overleaf.)

See Capital Cycle diagram overleaf.

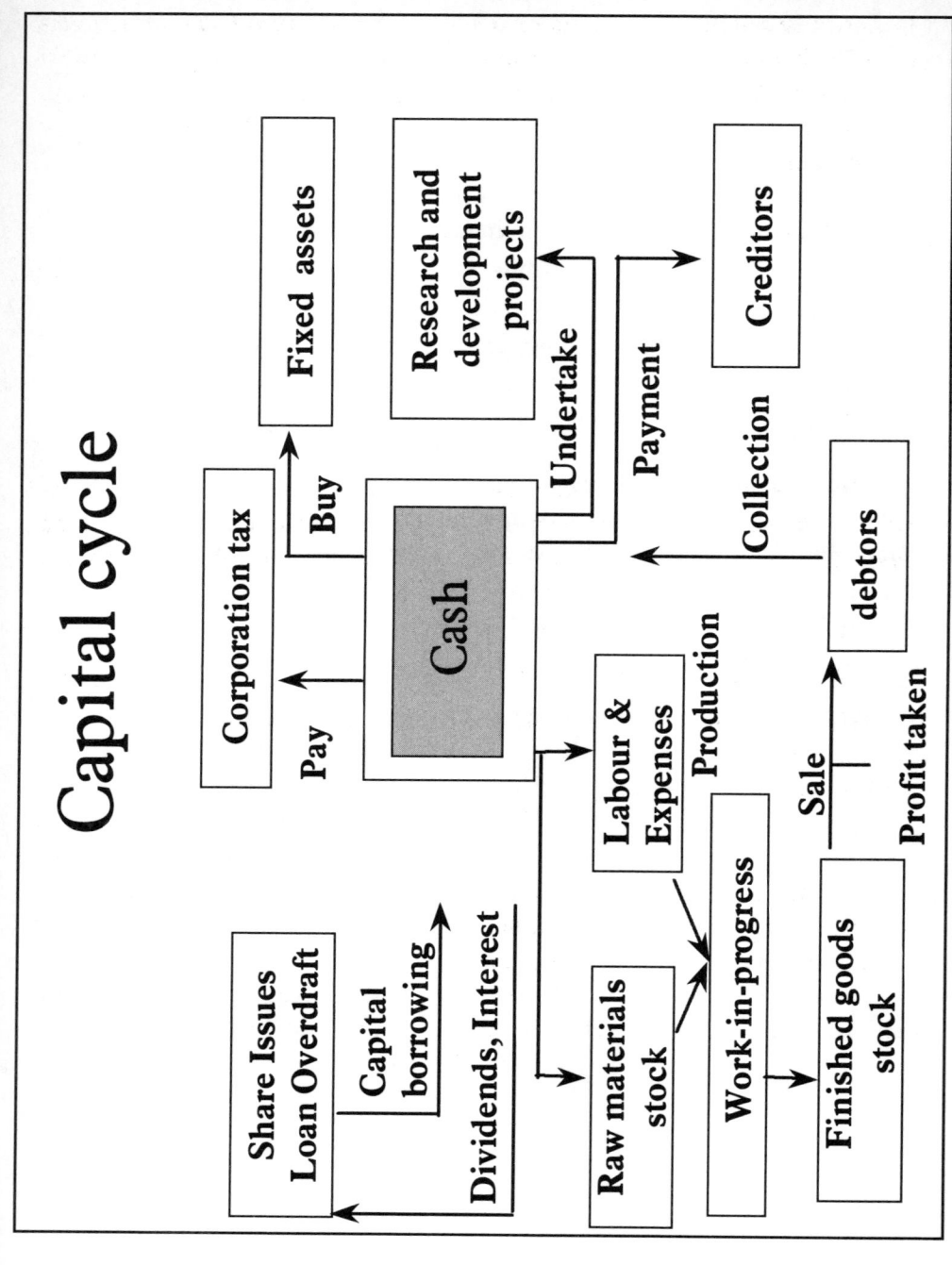

Cash can be seen, in the illustration opposite, as the central hub of the capital cycle. Cash is needed to continually finance the asset conversion cycle, to enable payments to the bank, to pay dividends to the shareholders, to pay taxes due, to purchase further fixed assets, and to undertake research and development, etc.

Cash flow is essentially uncertain and difficult to predict in that it is based to begin with on the projections of future operating income, and this is dependent on a number of important environmental factors, such as:

- The fundamental nature of the differing business sectors and the key risks to be managed within the sector both locally and globally.
- The current trends, both adverse and favourable, in the legal and regulatory environment surrounding the sector.
- The current competitive trends and changes within the sector

When we have considered the effects of these influences on a macro basis, we are then in an improved position to examine the more specific factors relating to the effect on the cash flows, such as the market position of the company and the business strategy that the management propose to follow.

Business Sector Fundamentals

A Corporate Manager in his assessment of corporate cash flow will inevitably, as part of the overall analysis, need to understand the company's competitive position, its strategy, and its resultant business risk effect on cash flow needs.

Every company has a strategy, be it express or implied. Express strategy is normally well defined and the result of a structured planning process. Implied strategy on the other hand is the result of different business units pursuing different (and sometimes conflicting) strategies. The combined result is very often unclear and can cause severe cash flow distortions.

A good starting point in the assessment of corporate risk is to undertake a general review on how the corporate's strategy has been formulated.

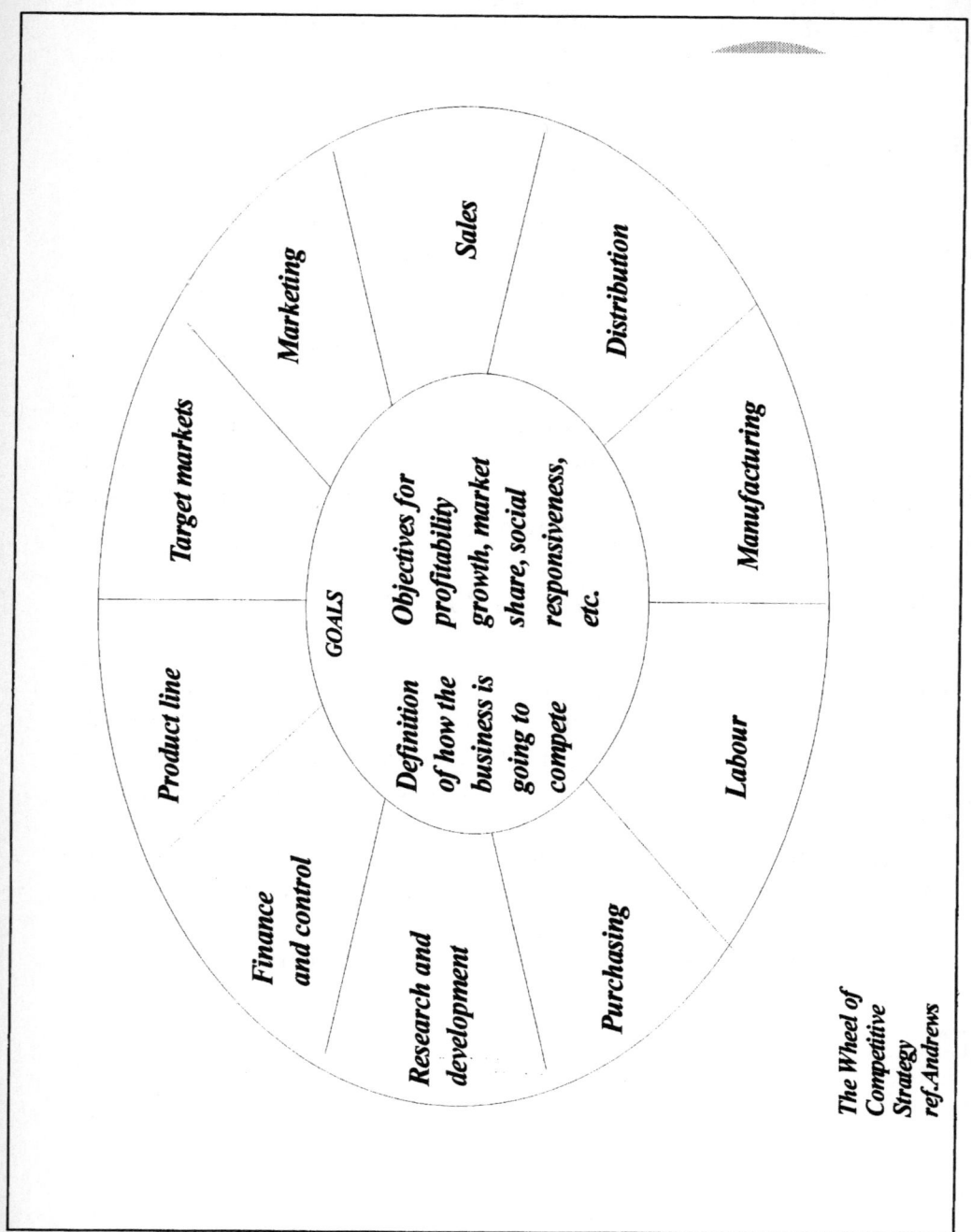

The Wheel of Competitive Strategy
ref-Andrews

The Wheel of Competitive Strategy

The Wheel of Competitive Strategy is a device for expressing the main aspects of a corporate's competitive strategy in summary format. The centre illustrates the corporate objectives and then goes on to state how the corporate is going to compete. The spokes of the wheel are operational factors by which the corporate intends to achieve the "centre" objectives. Within each spoke a summarized statement of intent is required. The designer of this wheel concept states that "for the corporate to progress effectively, not only must the policies radiate from the centre, but also each of the spokes must link smoothly together".

The next step is ask **what considerations are needed in formulating the centre statements for the wheel?**

The most frequently used model is to undertake a **SWOT analysis.**

SWOT stands for **S**trengths, **W**eaknesses, **O**pportunities and **T**hreats. In carrying out this type of assessment of strengths and weaknesses, we are undertaking an internal audit of the corporate and in evaluating opportunities and threats we are then carrying out an external review of the market place in which the corporate is currently operating.

Industry Identification

As part of this review of the company's individual strategies the Manager must analyse in depth the industry within which the company operates to identify its particular characteristics, features and peculiar risk profiles. The industry structure has a strong influence in determining the competitive rules of the game - as well as the strategies potentially available to the corporate. Outside forces usually affect all corporates in the industry, and therefore another key is the corporate's ability to deal with external factors. The intensity of competition within the industry is determined by industry economics as well as the strategies of current competitors.

A well-known model for looking at industry competition is Porter's Five Forces Model, which is a framework for identifying the collective strength or weaknesses of the factors driving industry competition. The intensity of the forces then in turn drive the rates of return on capital employed. For example, in industries such as tyres, paper and steel there is high intensity of competition and therefore economics dictate a low return on capital employed. Examples of relatively mild intensity are oil field equipment, cosmetics and toiletries, which generate high returns.

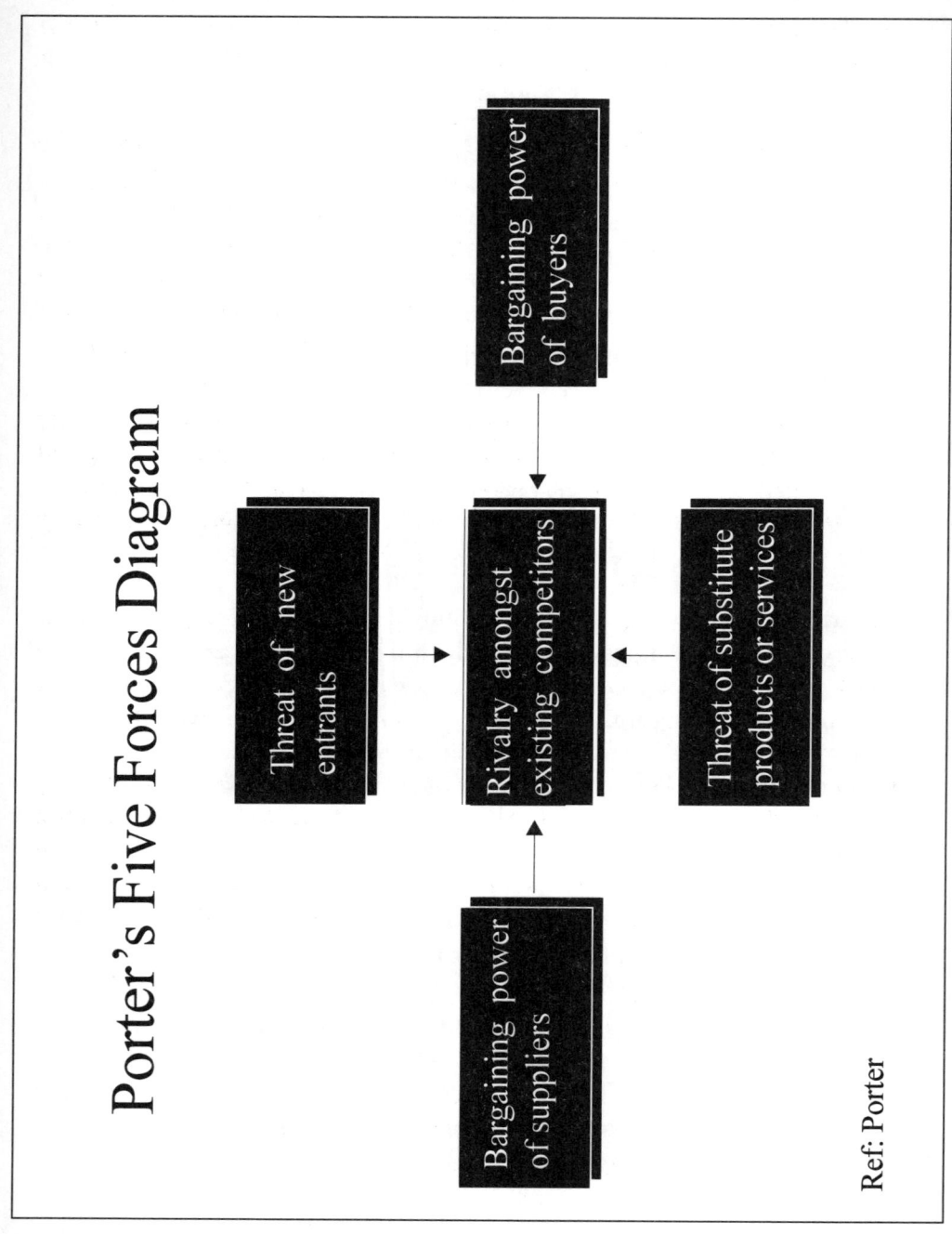

Porters Five Forces Model

The five forces to be considered are the external aspects of the bargaining power of buyers, the bargaining power of suppliers, the threat of new entrants, the threat of substitute products or services, and the internal forces (consisting of competitors within the industry being examined).

- **Knowledge of Sources of Competitive Pressure** - This provides the corporate with the ground work to develop a strategic action plan. Competitive pressures highlight the critical strengths and weaknesses of the company and also pinpoint the company position within an industry. Additionally, it highlights areas that promise to hold the most significance in terms of opportunities and threats to the corporate. The corporate then needs to decide on what strategic changes can be possible to take advantage of the opportunities or indeed to defend against external threats.
- **Barriers to Entry** - Economies of scale tend to deter entrants to the industry by forcing the entrant to come in on a very large scale or to accept a significant cost disadvantage within the industry (for example, mainframe computers). Product differentiation or brand identification creates a barrier by forcing potential entrants to spend heavily to overcome existing customer loyalty (for example in the sports shoe industry).

  Another barrier to entry could be the significant capital investment requirements and advertising programmes that can be needed to carry out an entry programme and this will in turn require large financial resources together with capital for current asset investment.
- **The Bargaining Power of Buyers** - Buyers compete within the industry by forcing down prices and trying to bargain for more services at a higher quality. This in turn leads to more competition within the industry – all of this at the expense of industry profitability. The power of the industry's important buying groups depends on a number of characteristics within the market situation and on the relative importance of purchases from the industry in the context of the overall business size.
- **The Bargaining Power of Suppliers** - Suppliers can in fact exert power over participants within an industry by threatening to raise prices or reduce the quality of purchased goods and services. Suppliers with great power can squeeze profitability out of an industry which is unable to recover cost increases by increasing its own prices. An example is chemical companies which have contributed to the erosion of profitability of contract aerosol packaging because the packages are facing intense competition from self-

manufacture by their buyers; accordingly they have limited freedom to raise their prices.

In conclusion of this five-force model, the use of this type of structural analysis can help to identify a large number of factors that can potentially have an impact on industry competition. The resulting analysis from the framework is therefore a useful tool to the corporate manager towards his or her assessment of corporate risk and its subsequent effect on cash flow issues. We can now progress to product strategies.

Three Principal Strategies

Depending on the corporate's positioning with regard to its strategic advantage and its strategic target, generic strategies tend to fall into three principal types: overall cost leadership, differentiation, and focus. See the diagram opposite.

- **Overall Cost Leadership** - This type of strategy requires a rigorous pursuit of cash flow efficiencies in terms of costs and overheads, volume and efficient systems. Therefore, it is essential that very close managerial attention be given in order to achieve these efficiency aims. Achieving a low-cost position gives defence against competitors and businesses will still obtain profitable returns, although quite fine. It also provides a defence against buyer power trying to force down prices and generally gives a favourable position from which to defend against low-cost substitute products or new entrants to the market. Examples in Britain include Black and Decker and Amstrad.
- **Differentiation** - The strategy of differentiation absorbs cash flow and requires the creation of differentiation in terms of the product or service offered by the business. Some examples of design or brand images include Mercedes Cars, Porsche Cars, Caterpillar Construction Equipment. Adopting a differentiation strategy should lead in turn to an ability to earn above average returns within an industry. Differentiation should also prove to be a defence against rivals, provided there is customer loyalty to the brand image of the particular corporate.
- **Focus** - This entire strategy is built around servicing a particular target and all functional policies are developed with this objective in mind. An effective and efficient service to the target is necessary for success relative to competitors who are generally competing more broadly. A focussed strategy can adopt a low-cost position for its strategic target (as shown in the diagram) or differentiation or a combination of both. The flow requirements can therefore be mixed.

Products and Markets
Three generic strategies

	STRATEGIC ADVANTAGE	
	Uniqueness perceived by the customer	Low cost position
S T R A T E G I C T A R G E T — Industry Wide	Differentation	Overall cost leadership
S T R A T E G I C T A R G E T — Particular Segment only	Focus	Focus

Ref: Porter

Business Sector Classification

The table below summarizes all the headings used in the equity page of the *Financial Times* to classify different shares into sectors.

Banks Merchant	Leisure & Hotels
Banks Retail	Life Assurance
Breweries	Media
Building & Construction	Oil Exploration & Production
Building Mats & Merchants	Oil Integrated
Chemicals	Other Financial
Distributors	Other Services & Businesses
Diversified Industrials	Paper Packaging & Printing
Electricity	Pharmaceuticals
Electronic & Electrical Equipment	Property
Engineering	Retailers, Food
Engineering, Vehicles	Retailers, General
Extractive Industries	Spirits, Wines & Ciders
Food Producers	Support Services
Gas Distributors	Telecommunications
Health Care	Textiles & Apparel
Household Goods	Tobacco
Insurance	Transport
Investment Trusts	Water
Investment Companies	

Clearly there are too many sectors here to consider the precise cash-flow dynamics of each one. What we need are methods of analysis that will give us insight as to the business risks of the different sectors and that assist us in our cash-flow planning. For example, in highly developed markets it is becoming less of a trend to run a variety of unrelated different businesses in groups (which are usually known as conglomerates). There are a number of reasons put forward for this:

- As no synergy exists between the businesses under common ownership there is no additional benefit to be gained from being a member of a group of unrelated businesses. There may be disadvantages because of issues such as a lack of new capital for investment due to cash surpluses being directed elsewhere, restrictions on expansion and group bureaucracy. These cash constraints possibly result in under-performance and the loss of potentially favourable opportunities for expansion.

- There are doubts that it is possible for one group of managers to have sufficient understanding of the real complexities and competitive dynamic of a variety of different businesses under their control. Corporate finance theory offers us the insight that there is no need for conglomerates to diversify their sources of cash flow to lower the specific risk of the group by operating in a variety of different industries or sectors because investors can achieve exactly the same diversification through the construction of an appropriate portfolio invested in the equity of a variety of different businesses. Indeed it is probably more expensive for the conglomerate to perform the diversification function.

There could be considerable cash flow benefits from floating or demerging businesses so that they stand alone, these being:

- Increased focus on their particular niche within the sector.
- Incentives and rewards tailored to the particular circumstances faced by the industry.
- The possibility of achieving an increased P/E ratio, and a more appropriate share price when compared to their original parent which will reflect the growth and earnings opportunities available from the particular business and make acquisitions paid for using equity comparatively cheaper.
- Easier access to funds by tapping equity markets directly, and by carrying levels of debt appropriate to the default risk of the sector in which the businesses are operating.

However, at present, conglomerates do continue to dominate less developed and developing countries. Some reasons for this are:

- A possible lower maturity level of business skills and education within the population places a premium on people with entrepreneurial talents, who can then operate on a broader front.
- The lack of social provision in the event of unemployment or sickness makes employment by larger industrial groups relatively more attractive to the employed than in more developed countries.
- Access to capital and business development skills is generally more difficult, so favouring larger groups with established positions.

Probably the most significant difference between the two environments is the level and intensity of competition. Whereas developed countries enjoy better infrastructure, communications and social provision when compared with lesser developed countries, there are also far more competitive markets in which to compete. Focus on a particular market or sector is therefore a far more important ingredient in achieving success.

The reason for the discussion of the relative merits is that, in examining the sector risk and cash flows of a group, we are actually seeking to examine the sector risk of a number of different and unique businesses within the group. For analysis purposes a group is therefore best viewed as a portfolio of different businesses, each of which has a different sector risk and cash flow profiles. Indeed a business with a divisional structure may be operating different profit centres, each of which faces entirely different levels of business risk and encounters varying cash flows. It is essential to go down to the level of each subsidiary in order to appreciate the real risks being managed. Attempting to perform a review of business risk by treating a diversified conglomerate as one business is unlikely to capture the real risk and cash flow dynamics of the group.

Cash Flow and the Stages of the Cycle (Product, Market or Company)

Stage of the Cycle	Development	Growth	Shake-out	Maturity	Oversupply	Decline	Extinction
Market Growth Rate	Minimal	High	High but slowing	GDP growth rate	Population growth	Negative	Strongly negative
Number of Segments	Very few	Few	Some	Many	Many	Less	Few
Technology Change in Product	Very large	Large	Large but slowing	Minimal	Minimal, or breakthrough	Minimal	None
Technology Change in Production Process	Minimal	Great	Very large	Large	Average	Minimal	None
Functional Emphasis	R & D	Engineering	Production	Marketing Distribution & Finance	Marketing Distribution & Finance	Marketing Finance	Marketing & Finance

Ref: Kotler

When we use this type of analysis, for many new products the development phase can take many years and usually incorporates negative cashflows – in the case of new drugs it can be over a decade. The most important thing about development is that it has some sort of market focus and careful cash management. Many people and organizations are inventive, and thousands of new ideas are patented every year. Regrettably though only a small fraction of these ideas ever make it into the market place, largely because this is the hardest part of the whole process.

The safest way to innovate is to determine what customers want and then to make it. A market-led approach at least ensures that there will be demand for the product when it is available, but even then there can be problems in achieving a low enough price at the initial volumes for the product to be competitive with near substitutes or the next best existing solution.

Generally, it is difficult to obtain debt finance in a new product (or business) because this is the highest business risk phase of the whole life cycle. Most innovation and R & D is therefore financed with *cash* coming from equity of some form of private capital.

There are a number of challenges for management in this phase, such as:

- Satisfying demand for the product by establishing volume manufacturing facilities
- Developing the product to drive down its cost, and to improve its performance and attractiveness for the consumer
- Re-engineering the product to make it easier and cheaper to manufacture
- Managing the critical stages of the cash flow

The key to success in this phase is maintaining the cash and the attractiveness of the product to consumers so as to hold as much market share as possible. It is in this phase that the competition can arrive. Having noticed the attractiveness of the product, other businesses with the capability to manufacture it start to offer similar products of their own. This is where protected market positions are so valuable; in the drugs industry patent protection prevents other pharmaceutical companies from copying the product until patent protection expires. Patent protection is valuable, as are unique processes of manufacture which cannot be purchased from suppliers of process machinery or rely on a unique formula of some kind which involves extensive research to replicate. A good example is Intel's dominance in the microprocessor chip market.

If the product is priced so as to make the maximum returns there is a risk that a competitor will sell its version of the product at a lower price to acquire market share, which it can then exploit for the rest of the life of the product. Retaining market share in this phase is the most important objective.

The growth phase also incorporates negative cash flows and attracts competitors into the market. The larger the market the more interest there will be in entering it. While the rate of growth continues to increase there are plenty of customers for everybody and all participants who are remaining competitive should experience growth and make profits.

However, when the rate of growth starts to slow there are now too many competitors chasing too few customers. The winners in this phase are therefore those who have established some form of competitive advantage over their rivals. A competitive advantage is some advantage unique to the business enjoying it which other competitors do not have. Typical forms of competitive advantage are:

- Market share, which should translate into the most potent advantage of all: lower costs and therefore cheaper selling prices. This is why maintaining market share is so important. In many industries it confers on the dominant business the opportunity to create larger economies of scale than their competitors. Once you have created a growth market you must grow with it or risk losing control of the market to a competitor.
- Distinctive product features attractive to the consumer
- Distinctive designs attractive to the consumer
- Proprietary production techniques
- Unique geographical advantages
- Unique patent rights or intellectual property
- Control of distribution
- Branding

Businesses that have failed to develop a reasonable market share, or develop different forms of competitive advantage, could exit in this phase. This can be by bankruptcy due to lack of cash flow, simply because they are not able to match the economies of scale of their larger competitors, or by takeover, which is more likely as the market share already achieved will be valuable to a competitor, if it can be retained after acquiring the competitor. So we observe increasing supplier rationalization in the shake-out phase, with the total number of businesses manufacturing a particular product or active in a particular market segment declining in number.

The shake-out phase ends when the market goes "ex-growth", meaning that the market is now considered mature. It may still be growing at a modest rate due to technical innovation, fashion and the replacement market, but we are now at the position where everyone who wants one of the product has already acquired one. In developed economies a television set is an example of a mature product.

The businesses that are left at this stage are typically few and large, but this does not mean that there is no room for niche players, which concentrate on the premium or luxury end of the market. However they will not be volume producers.

The dominant businesses are typically global suppliers of the product in question. Their main objective in this phase is to hold market share. As both the product and the technology used to produce it are now relatively settled, the emphasis in management switches from innovation and growth to marketing (particularly branding and financial control). Maintaining a low cost base is now essential because higher costs will result in losses and negative operating cash flows due to the highly competitive nature of the mature product market place. There are no new entrants at this stage because the costs of entry and the learning curve involved in achieving market levels of efficiency are too high to justify entry. There is also the problem of achieving consumer recognition in an already mature and crowded market place.

The dominant businesses now seek to defend their market share by using a variety of techniques, as follows:

- Branding to establish a preference in the mind of the consumer. This includes the use of a large advertising and promotional budget as a source of competitive advantage.
- Product proliferation to confuse the consumer makes it more difficult to compare price and performance and create a barrier to entry to dissuade new competitors from entering. This is a technique refined to perfection in the washing powder business, where there are only two main suppliers.
- Constant new product introductions to keep the product's appearance fresh and new, achieved by constantly compressing the development cycle, a technique refined to a source of competitive advantage by Japanese manufacturers.
- Control of distribution to make it more difficult for new entrants to reach consumers.
- Use of a variety of distribution channels, including retail, petrol stations, vending machines, mail order, telephone shopping, agents, distributors, etc.

The final part of the life cycle concerns the decline and disappearance of the product or market. This is an inevitable process, because of the endless process of change which is taking place in every society that exploits technology.

What are the problems and cash flow issues inherent in the decline phase? The first problem is recognizing that a market is actually in decline. Unsurprisingly most managers tend to disbelieve that the product they and their predecessors have been making and selling for so long is now being superseded by another technology or substitute. They therefore may adopt the wrong management behaviour by continuing to invest cash flow aggressively in new product development and marketing and by believing any downward trend in sales is temporary. Perhaps the appropriate behaviour in this phase is to recognize the reality of the changes, and if unable to respond by competing in the new changed market place manage an organized retrenchment and decline as the available market shrinks. This phase can be enormously cash generative as, in addition to generating cash from operations, the company is able to recover the cash invested in working capital and fixed assets such as factories and machinery. The managerial emphasis is therefore on financial control to maximize the returns achieved from the withdrawal. Selling prices may actually start to rise again in this phase as competition withdraws and the product becomes more scarce for those who still require it.

Cash Flow and the Value Chain

Business in the Value Chain	Typical Business/Cash Flow Features
Bauxite Mine	Commodity pricing, capital intensive
Shipper	Commodity pricing, low margin
Aluminium Smelter	Commodity pricing, capital, energy cost driven
Road Haulier	Commodity pricing, labour costs, capital
Rolling Mill	Location, operating costs, technology
Road Haulier	Commodity pricing, labour costs
Stockholder	Location, operating costs, service offer
Fabricator	Service offer, low capital need
Installer	Reliability offer, low capital need

As an example, aluminium starts its life as a ore in the ground. Recovered using mining and quarrying techniques, the ore is typically loaded into ships and taken to an aluminium smelter. Using enormous amounts of electricity the smelter converts the ore to a large ingot of aluminium. This is then transported to a rolling mill for conversion into sheet and bar. The aluminium is bought by a metal stockholder, who sells the aluminium bar to an extruder who extrudes the aluminium bar into a section. This is purchased by a fabricator who cuts the section and assembles it, together with other components, into a patio door. The installer, who ordered the door from the fabricator, then installs the door for the end user.

There are therefore nine businesses in the value chain all using cash between the aluminium in the ground and the end user. Each business could not be more different, located in different countries. For example, the bauxite might come from Jamaica, be shipped across the Atlantic to an aluminium smelter in Northern France, then travel to a rolling mill in the Netherlands before being transported by road transport to a British metal stockholder, who services a fabricator in Wembley, who sells to an installer in Wimbledon! As world trade continues to develop, such journeys are now commonplace with quite low-value

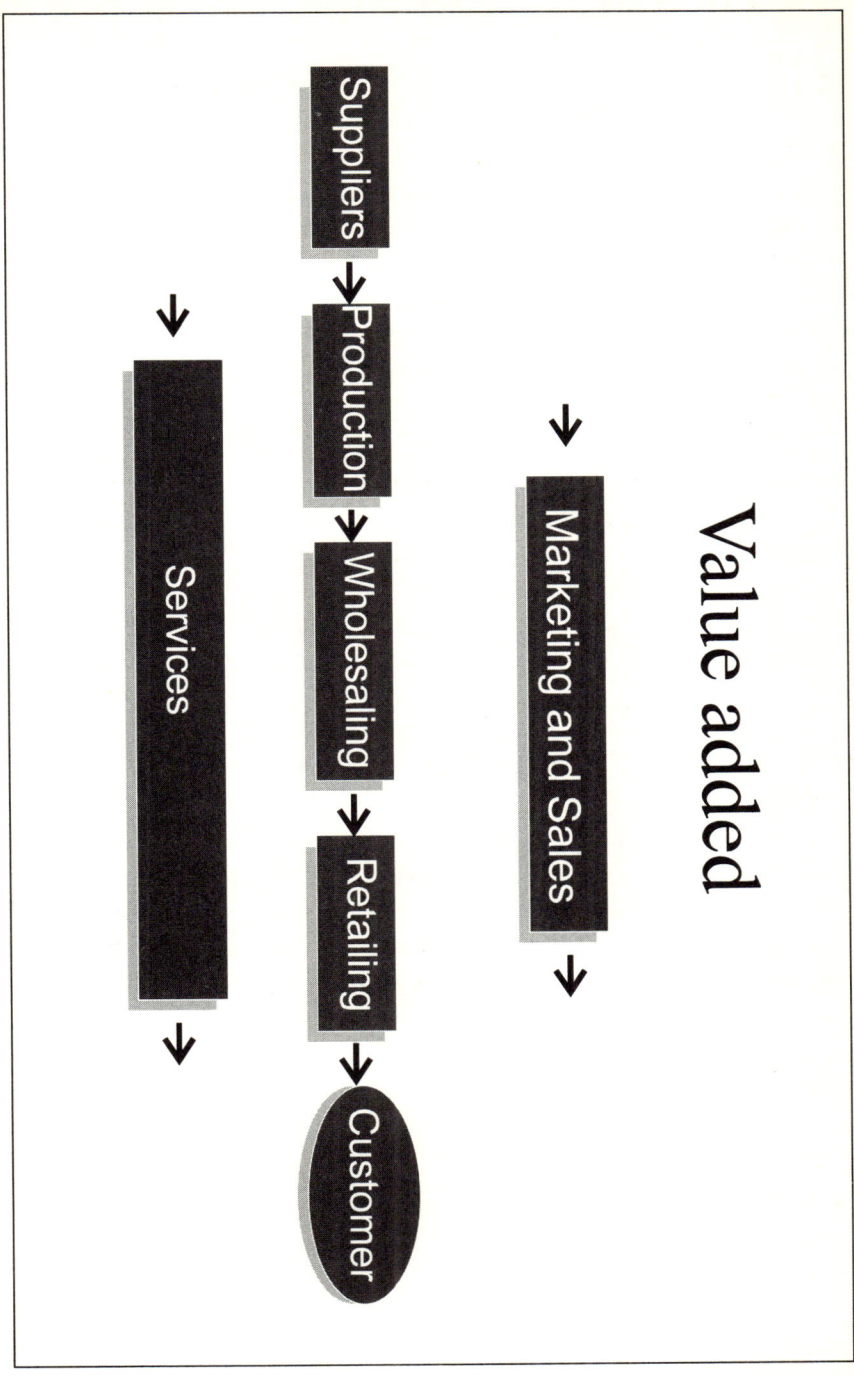

goods travelling huge distances. This globalization is driven by the efficiency of the industries involved. In earlier times it was simply not economic to move goods long distances because of the costs involved in so doing; the invention of the steam and petrol engine changed things dramatically. International trade continues to become more efficient as newer technology's storage, such as containerization, continue to lower costs.

Understanding the implications of the position in the value chain can provide valuable insights as to the business risk and cash flow dynamics of that particular position. One of the most curious aspects of value chain analysis is that extremely successful and profitable businesses can be adjacent in the chain to highly competitive, nightmare business sectors where profitability and returns are elusive and unpredictable, with a high rate of business failures. Understanding who in the chain manages to extract the most and the least added value from the product on its way to the end user tells us much about the risk.

The aluminium smelter is, of course, very capital-intensive consuming large amounts of cash flow, typically costing more than £100 million to construct. Its profitability depends on access to low-cost energy sources and proximity to markets. All the other things that a smelter can do to lower costs and enhance performance can be copied by its competitors. Its output, aluminium, is a commodity; prices are therefore not under the control of the smelter but are determined by global supply and demand for aluminium. If costs are lower than world norms the smelter will be profitable. The output can be sold anywhere in the world there is demand for aluminium, subject only to the cost of transportation, so the business is not particularly exposed to the economic cycle risk of local economies, although there will be a transport cost advantage in supplying local users. Business risk is therefore partly driven by the location and cost of the inputs to the smelting process, the most important of which is the cost of electricity.

In contrast the installer is typically a small business which gains customers from advertising and reputation. With little capital required there are minimal barriers to entry and hence competition is fierce. So understanding value chains is an important skill to acquire and will assist us in the cash flow planning process. Experienced manufacturing managers, when shown a new and unfamiliar product, can often analyse the inherent added value simply be examining the components and processes involved in arriving at the product. Their relative complexity and difficulty of manufacture determine the value added available to the relevant supplier.

Cash Flow and Developing Markets and Products

Moving a business forward from its present position by taking some sort of new initiative incorporates different levels of risk. Markets can be:

- Fragmented
- Specialized (or luxury)
- Stalemate
- Volume

Fragmented markets are characterized by the following features:

- A large variety of competitors and products on offer
- The need for constant incremental innovation in order to remain competitive
- They are relatively labour intensive
- They are low-skill based
- They use available bought-in technology
- They require a design or research and development function
- They are working-capital driven

Examples of fragmented markets are textiles, retailing, distribution, wood and metal fabrication, agriculture and creative businesses. They represent a relatively high business risk because they are all businesses in which it is difficult to achieve sustainable competitive advantages; any competitive advantage tends to be temporary because it is usually easily copied by rivals. Advantage stems typically from better designs, better technology for production and better marketing.

Specialized (or luxury) markets are characterized by the following features:

- Small, defined markets
- A high-value offer
- Few competitors
- Quality driven
- The purchase is highly discretionary for the consumer

Examples of specialized markets are exotic motor cars, perfumes, *haute couture*, Swiss watches, and other very high-value luxury products. Businesses such as Ferrari, Aston Martin, Cartier, Chanel, Bollinger and Wedgewood are all in this market. Businesses offering ultra-exotic technologies also might fall in this category, such as carbon-fibre bicycles. They usually enjoy high margins generating strong cash flow, but most of this is reinvested in maintaining the level of excellence required in order to be competitive. The main risk is that of recession, when spending on all luxury and exotic goods declines dramatically.

Stalemate markets are characterized by the following features:

- Commodity products
- Mature markets
- Pricing driven by market supply and demand
- No dominant competitor
- Utilization of available process and manufacturing technology
- The scale of economies is limited by technical issues.
- Raw materials represent the highest input costs.

Examples of stalemate markets are the manufacture of bulk chemicals, textile fibres, oil refining, agri-product processing and paper making. The risks and cash flows involved are again primarily cyclical, with over-capacity in times of weak demand being the main problem.

Volume markets are characterized by the following features:

- Mass markets
- Standardized products
- A discretionary purchase for the customer
- Major economies of scale available to large producers
- Mass distribution to all outlets in the market
- Few dominant competitors

Examples of volume markets are food and drink, and other consumer products such as household consumables retailed in fast-moving consumer goods outlets such as supermarkets. The risks are of loss of market share or margin because of changes in competition, distribution or consumer preferences.

Recognizing the type of market in which the businesses being analysed is involved tells us much about the significant risks and subsequent cash flows being faced by the business. By examining other businesses involved in that type of market, we are able to recognize the distinctive features which make businesses relatively more successful and the distinctive nature of the risks inherent in operating in that sector.

These cash flow and risk variables can be influenced by:

- Technological problems or breakthrough
- Substitute products developed by competitors or a new product developed by the company
- Product cannot satisfy regulatory requirements, or a regulatory breakthrough is made
- Economic recession or boom

The business cycle results from the nature of a company's product and the cash flow dynamics and risks involved in creating and selling the product. To understand business cycles in detail we therefore need to understand the process through which companies create and use cash. A manufacturing company's normal operating activity is that cash is used to buy raw materials; this action creates accounts payable. Cash is needed for labour costs and overheads to provide goods for resale. Goods are then sold, normally giving rise to debtors on credit terms. When these accounts are settled, the business ends up with cash again, hopefully more than at the beginning of the cycle. Reviewing this business cycle will help us:

- To develop an understanding of the cash flow risks that business are exposed to at different stages of the operating process
- To understand the process by which businesses consume and generate cash at the operating level
- To gain an appreciation of the financing needs of the business, and to evaluate if financing is structured appropriately for the business
- To gain an appreciation of the investment requirements of the business and to evaluate the investment decisions that are appropriate for the business

The risk inherent in a company with a long operating cycle is greater than one with a short cycle. The longer the period between the purchase of raw materials and the collection of cash from the buyer of finished goods, the more time there is for cash flow difficulties to develop.

Also, a long cycle usually implies:

- More investment in fixed assets
- More cash required
- More value added so higher risk associated with, for example, labour
- Higher return demanded by shareholders to compensate for higher risk: there is therefore a need for higher margins

The reverse is true for a short cycle as seen in commodity traders, who have high turnover, little capital, minimal value added and thin profit margins.

Business cycles, as we have all seen within our experience, vary from one industry to another and among firms in the same industry. Food processors and grocery retailers are frequently given as examples of industries with lower working investment risks, whereas cyclical manufacturing industries, such as steel, are regarded as having especially high working investment risk. Surely, a key reason for being in business is to generate more cash at the end of the cycle than there was at the beginning through the added value of producing a product for which there is a market demand. However, if prices of inputs, costs and finished goods change then this cycle could become loss making. If a company manages the cycle inefficiently by holding raw materials for long periods of time, allowing long payment periods from debtors but paying creditors more quickly than necessary, then the cycle may also become loss making (known as negative operating cash flow). Other situations in which negative operating cash flow can arise include a company which is growing very quickly, therefore investing large amounts of cash in stocks and debtors in order to meet large orders. Declining companies or companies in recession by contrast can often "throw off" cash as a result of running down existing stock and not purchasing new stock to replace it.

The challenge for all managers of companies is to run the cycle as quickly as possible on a continuing basis in order to maximize the sustainable growth rates that the business can achieve. Sustainable growth rates can be calculated approximately by the use of formulae such as the one illustrated opposite together with an example calculation.

Reviewing Variables

- **Demand variability:** The more stable the demand for a company's products (other things held constant) the lower the company's cash flow risk.
- **Sales price variability:** Companies whose products are sold in highly volatile markets are exposed to more cash flow risk than similar companies whose output prices are relatively stable.
- **Input price variability:** Companies whose inputs are highly uncertain are exposed to a high degree of business risk.
- **Ability to adjust output prices for changes in input prices:** Some companies have little difficulty in raising their own output prices when input costs rise, and the greater the ability to adjust output prices, the lower the degree of cash flow risk. This factor is especially important during periods of high inflation.

Sustainable Growth Rate

The sustainable growth rate test can be used to give approximation of the level of sales growth a company can sustain without resorting to increased external liabilities.

Probably the best known formula is:

$$G = \frac{P(1-D)(1+L)}{T - [P(1-D)(1+L)]} \times 100$$

Where
- G = Sustainable Growth Rate
- P = Profit after Tax/Sales
- D = Dividends/Profits after tax
- L = Total Liabilities/Equity
- T = Total Assets/Sales

Ref: Boyadjian & Warren

Sustainable Growth Rates An Example:

	#000s
Sales	247,793
Profit After Tax	789
Dividends	122
To Retained Earnings	667
Total Assets	184,781
Total Liabilities	99,237
Net Worth	85,544
L = $\dfrac{99,237}{85,544}$ =	1.16
Sustainable Growth Rate	0.8%

- **The extent to which costs are fixed (operating leverage):** If a high percentage of a company's costs are fixed and hence do not decline when demand falls off, it increases the company's cash flow risk. This factor is called **operating leverage**, and it is discussed earlier under margin of safety.

Although each of these factors are determined largely by the company's industry characteristics, each is also controllable to some extent by management. For example, most companies can, through their marketing policies, take actions to stabilize both unit sales and sales prices. However, this stabilization may require either large expenditure on advertising or price concessions to induce customers to commit to purchasing fixed quantities at fixed prices in the future. Similarly, firms can reduce the volatility of future input costs by negotiating long-term labour and materials supply contracts, but they may have to agree to pay prices above the current price level to obtain these contracts.

The relationships between suppliers, buyers and competitors therefore shapes a company's terms of trade – i.e., how quickly it pays suppliers, collects cash from customers and turns its raw materials into finished goods.

All of these variables and the previous comment on life cycles, value chains etc. can be examined much more closely by looking in detail at a case study of a corporate facing significant demand variables, economic cycles and the effect on its cash flows.

In Conclusion

The purpose of this chapter is to create an awareness of business risk and its impact on cash flow requirements. A good Corporate Manager must be able to analyse, identify and understand the company's specific strategy and the competition within the market place to determine cash flow needs and the appropriate financial structure and products to meet those needs.

2

CASE STUDY: ERF

An illustration of continuing strategic cash management through economic cycles

This case features a detailed analysis of careful cash management through the corporate history and business landmarks: the development of this truck business, from its foundation in 1933 to the culmination as a Plc and the last independent truck operator in the United Kingdom.

Part 1

Readers are encouraged to carry out a full review of the background to ERF's success from Edwin Richard Foden's "Vision" to the commencement of the 1980s. As you are reading the text, please look out for *key success factors both in terms of product development and cash flow management.*

Origin

ERF was born in the terrible shadow of the great depression of 1930. Convinced that steam power was obsolete and that Foden - the family firm - was already behind the times, Edwin Richard Foden and his son Dennis branched out on their own. They had decided that diesel-engined lorries, and not Foden's clanking steam dinosaurs, would pave the way forward.

It took courage and conviction to leave the business he had inherited from his father, but Edwin Richard had a vision. He had foreseen the death knell of the steam lorry in the closing days of World War I, and the 1930 Traffic Act (with its restrictive practices) merely reinforced his suspicions. Also, the insurance companies were baulking at the idea of underwriting welded steam boilers. He knew that times were changing. Foden's management did not share his forward thinking, however, and a boardroom wrangle ended with Edwin Richard "retiring" in 1932. Little did they know that by 1933 he would be back with a vengeance, fronting E R Foden and Son Diesel with his son Dennis.

Case Study: ERF

It was not long after his departure from Foden that neighbours began to notice lights burning through the night at Hilary House, the family home in Elworth. The ERF diesel lorry was being born in secret. Edwin Richard, at the age of 62, was fighting back with Dennis and two former colleagues: Ernest Sherratt, later to be chief designer and technical boss, and George Faulkner, who became works manager. "We worked in a lean-to conservatory," says Sherratt. "It was very comfortable, and not at all ramshackle" and by Easter 1933 the first ERF prototype was at the design stage. The company made its debut at The Motor Show in Olympia later the same year. "People didn't take us seriously. They said 'what can they do, just three men and a boy?' But we didn't worry," Sherratt recalls. "We just got cracking with a little factory on land rented from a local coachbuilder called Jennings. We could build six lorries at a time, and we were so busy getting the job right first time, we never bothered with a research and development department."

It was a two-axled six-tonner called the CI4 that started it all, and Edwin Richard wrote, in his very first sales brochure: "legislation has decided that the wagon must have an unladen weight of under four tons. Therefore my son and I have decided to manufacture a vehicle in this taxation class and have included the strongest frame, the most powerful engine, a robust gearbox, sturdy axles, coupled with efficient and powerful brakes." He saved the crunch for the end: "We are building this on totally different business methods which we know will reduce very considerably overhead charges, and in that way our customers will reap the benefit." The brave founders of ERF had not only gambled on a new company with a new product in difficult times: they had also decided to revolutionize the way vehicle manufacturers went about things.

To minimize the cash outlay and to control the working capital cycle they bought in the components. It may sound simple enough today, but it was heresy at the time when industry leaders like Foden, Thorneycroft, Albion, AEC, Leyland *et al* made everything in their own foundries and machine shops. "That was our key difference, and time has proved us right," says Sherratt. "We could switch supplies around by buying in." The axles came from Kirkstall; the cabs were put together by Jennings; the engine was the four-cylinder 4LW Gardner; and David Brown supplied a four-speed transmission. The Company did, however, make its own radiators out of aluminium. The braking system used the then-new vacuum-hydraulic principle, with Lockheed supplying the hydraulics and Clayton Dewandre the servos. The first chassis was supplied on 1 September 1933, just six months after the company's birth. More models were to follow, and customers soon began to sense that ERF was a badge worth following. Haulage in the thirties was even tougher than it is today. One early customer told the company, "The day I can't overload an ERF, I'll stop buying them." ERF won a reputation for strength and the small family of firms which bought ERF in the beginning were soon joined by big fleet buyers like Reliance Tankers.

At the end of 1933 ERF had made 31 trucks and had redefined the seven- to eight-ton load capacity concept in British commercial vehicle design. Production reached 96 vehicles in 1934; 115 in 1935; 210 in 1936; 352 in 1937; 413 in 1938; 434 in 1939 and 427 at the end of the decade. In just seven hectic years ERF's annual production rate had increased fourteen-fold.

Meanwhile in 1935 ERF built its first six-wheeler – made to order for Hall's Toffee. "That was rather funny, actually," Ernest Sherratt recalls. "Hall's ordered our first six-wheeler and Reliance Tankers the second, and while we were building the latter they came back and said 'could you make it an eight-wheeler?' We did, of course." That year was a watershed in other ways. The original company name, E R Foden and Son Diesel, was causing confusion, claimed Sandbach neighbours Foden, and ERF was born as the official marque name. It was also the beginning of the run-up to World War II. The line-up of a 4x2, 6x4, 8x4 and twin-steer 6x2 were all in production. Simple and strong, the CI4 truck that had been present at the company's birth was also its sole product for the Ministry of Supply at the start of the war. The beginning of World War II meant that ERF's designs for future trucks had to go on the back burner. Tough times had bred a tough competitor, and ERF's sturdy little truck was fighting its way forward on all fronts. Designer Ernest Sherratt, however, had other ideas and he was already plotting the shape of things to come. War wastes so many things, not least progress, and ERF was just biding its time.

1940s

ERF built its 4x2 four-wheeler flagship right through to 1945 and the close of World War II, but wartime shortages meant that the army's preferred Gardner 4LW diesels could not be supplied in sufficient numbers to satisfy the ERF production lines: 400 chassis a year had been planned at the outset of the war and 434 were built in 1939/40, before the rot set in. Only 427 chassis were made in 1940/41 and 360 in 1941/2. This dwindled to 322 and 248 in the following two years with output down to 237 in 1944/5.

"We certainly did not make a lot of money out of the war," recalls Earnest Sherratt. For the first time in the company's short history, engines made by other suppliers were fitted to keep things moving as quickly as possible and help cash flow generation.

AEC 7.7-litre diesels, similar to those fitted in the Matador gun tractors, were used. The military took the Gardner-powered trucks; civilian buyers got the substitute vehicles. Standard CI4 units were used by the Royal Army Service

Case Study: ERF

Corps in the Normandy landings. The CI5 was powered by a five-cylinder Gardner diesel, the 5LW. It had appeared several years before the start of the war to suit operators unhappy with the power of the four-cylinder engine. While civilian and military ERF trucks shared the same basic design there were a number of differences on the latter - not least to its radiator grille: the army eschewed chrome in favour of paint. Headlamps were made smaller and had blackout cowls fitted. Side windows were opened by hand rather than by mechanism to reduce production costs. The most unusual modification to the military ERF was the fitting of a special detector plate at the front of the truck which changed colour in the presence of poison gas. Every soldier comes home from war with the memory of heroic deeds pinned like a medal over his heart. Their tales may grow taller in the telling, but are generally rooted in fact. Many tales from World War II include trucks. One involved a well-worn ERF working for the RASC in France, close to the action. It hit a mine which blew the vehicle clean into a neighbouring field, tearing the body from the chassis, puncturing the sump and ruining the tyres. The crew miraculously survived, to haul themselves and the remains of the truck's body back together again. They fixed up the sump, salvaged tyres from abandoned trucks and re-fitted the ERF for the road. The cargo of essential rations was gathered up from surrounding fields and thrown back on board. Within five hours the ERF was back in the war.

With annual production below the 250 mark at the end of the war, and steel rationing a fact of life for the foreseeable future, ERF had to battle on with the same dogged persistence and careful cash flow management. It was 1957 before the company could top its 1939 production total, after a long, slow slog through the grey years of post-war austerity. Lack of raw materials, finance and skilled men meant that any changes had to be kept to a minimum. Despite this CI4 and CI5 rigids sold well, as did the lightweight OE3 model which used the 3.8-litre Gardner 4LK diesel. As soon as the 4LK engine was available it was fitted and the model renamed LK44.

In 1948, however, a new and more rounded ERF appeared. It became known as the "Streamline" cab with its elaborate, curved grille and flush headlamps. Design boss Ernest Sherratt had put many years of frustration and delay into the new truck, along with more recent modifications like the 1946 arrival of an Eaton two-speed axle. The Streamline had a stronger chassis, better brakes, and was not built with an integral cab but with a curved dash plate which mirrored the line of the radiator. Customers could buy the chassis and fit their own coach-built cab if they did not want the ERF standard cab.

The 1940s closed with nationalization of the haulage industry and the creation of the forerunner of today's National Freight Consortium. The political move made no difference to ERF: it was already popular with British Road

Services (BRS), the company that would become the keystone of Britain's nationalized road transport market. Indeed, ERF was by now so well established, that no-one could think of it as a Johnny-come-lately. It was gearing up to take the truck world by storm with a radical truck design - but that tale belongs to the brighter era of the 1950s.

1950s

The death of Edwin Richard Foden in December 1950, at the age of 80, was a body blow the company, his family and the Sandbach workforce. He was admired for his acute business brain, renowned for his sense of humour and respected for his brand of leadership that had nurtured ERF's "family" atmosphere. Dennis became managing director and Peter Foden, then only 20, was made a director, ensuring that ERF would live on as a family concern.

The first three years of the decade were tough, with steel rationing remaining in force until 1953 and ERF struggling through the morass of death duties that had followed on from Edwin Richard's death. ***The cash flow solution was to go public and shares were offered in 1954,*** just after Peter left Sandbach for his two years' National Service in The Royal Electrical and Mechanical Engineers, where he was eventually commissioned and spent most of his time in Germany with the Sixth Armoured Division.

By the early fifties a new cab was emerging that would shape ERF's future and take it into the booming 1960s. Dennis shared his father's flair for design and had sensed that a radical change was needed. In 1952, prototypes of a new and rounded cab fronted by a small oval radiator grille began to appear. The profile of the cab front was about eight feet in radius and its unusual rounded shape led to the use of glass fibre panels for the first time. Chief designer Ernest Sherratt was delighted when he saw the new truck taking shape. "It was exciting," he says. "We were being adventurous, doing things that no-one had done before."

A young design engineer at Jennings called Gerald Broadbent was responsible for the distinctive flowing lines, and christened it the "Klear View", or KV cab. Today Gerald runs Boalloy, one of the country's most successful bodybuilders and trailer manufacturers, with the best-selling Tautliner design to its credit. "I still think that the KV cab is beautiful," says Sherratt. "The curved windscreen was Gerald's idea and the whole thing was my pride and joy when I first saw it. I still have to say to people, even now, that their cabs are too square and too box shaped. A little bit of curvature makes all the difference. Operators fell in love with the KV. It was far in advance of anything else on the market at that time - no doubt about it."

The Gardner engine was specified as the KV powerhouse and the truck became a legend. Many stayed on the road for more than 20 years, working hard until they dropped. "The chassis retained the post-war design," Sherratt recalls, "it only changed in minor detail." The KV first showed its elegant lines in 1956 and the Gardner 6LX diesel, which was to live on for years, first appeared in 1958. The KV and the 6LX immediately hit it off, driven through a six-speed David Brown gearbox. In the same year, however, a decision was made to offer customers more choice and different engine options. Purists moaned, of course, but Charlie Butts of Butts in Northampton leapt at the chance and took the first ERF KV eight-legger with a Cummins engine towards the end of 1958. This was the beginning of ERF's switch to Cummins, leading to the strong relationship that the two companies have today. An ICI quarry at Buxton took the first ERF KV with a Rolls Royce diesel at about the same time. A number of people at ERF felt that the operators were buying unnecessary horsepower, but it was now company policy and ERF knew what the customer wanted, the customer got. And that was that.

In August 1958 ERF fitted the first disc brakes to a heavy commercial vehicle - but they proved to be too expensive in service and were withdrawn in favour of more conventional drum brakes. The maximum gross vehicle weight in 1958 was 24 tons, but a 32-ton limit was just around the corner and better stopping power was going to prove a key ingredient to operating at higher GVWs. At the end of the 1950s no-one seemed to like artics, and drawbars were ruled out as uneconomical because the law required a brakeman inside the cab and alongside the driver at all times to brake the trailers. While the technology of disc brakes was still in need of development, their appearance on an ERF chassis was a further pointer to the company's ability to stay ahead of the game and dare to be different.

The KV pushed sales up and the 1959/60 annual production total reached the 500 mark for the first time in ERF's history. The KV was versatile enough to appear in a number of guises, most notably as a bonneted rigid, called the 54GSF. ERF nicknamed the snub-nosed beauty as "Sabrina" in light-hearted tribute to her resemblance to a film star of the era. Other manufacturers tried to emulate the streamlined, rounded appeal of the KV cab shape, but failed.

Its look today defines 1950s' style and design - quirky but utilitarian, futuristic and optimistic, imaginative and resourceful. After two hard and gloomy decades, the good times were coming. The late 1950s were happier times for ERF, and Ernest Sherratt recalls the era fondly. The Suez crisis and de-nationalization followed by re-nationalization were temporary but insignificant hiccups for the truck market, he says. "But we were making steady progress all the time, and we were making money. Peter took to the company like a duck to water, and the motor industry as a whole was booming." The 1960s were not going to be a let-down.

For the first eight years that mechanic George Hunt worked for Manchester Coop milk division, new trucks - and spares - were like gold dust. It was wartime, and Britain was concentrating its energies, including vehicle production, on winning the fight against Hitler. Hunt joined the Co-operative Wholesale Society's Rhyl operation as an apprentice in 1942, aged 16. No new trucks were being built, and pre-War ERF tankers were kept busy collecting milk from local dairies for delivery to the Midlands.

But the Gardner 5LW-engined three-tonners, with David Brown crash gearboxes, were tough. "We didn't have a lot of trouble," he recalls, "although we were keeping vehicles long after they should have been scrapped". "They were slow revving and did 200,000 miles (320,000km) before being stripped down. The more mass-produced Morris Commercials, which also ran, wouldn't do that." But there were problems. After 320,00km the Gardner engines became caked in grease, and Hunt remembers "digging with a shovel to get at the valves - there were no detergent oils in those days".

He served five years' apprenticeship and still works at the Rhyl depot, with three years to go to his retirement. "Mechanics then were more like craftsmen - they were pretty much able to do everything themselves." Because he had no experience of working before the War, Hunt accepted the lack of spare parts as normal. Make-do-and-mend even extended to welding broken valves. Occasionally he drove the ERFs as a relief man. The runs (maximum speed 30mph/48km/h) lasted from 7am until 3pm and took the trucks along narrow North Wales lanes. "The Co-op milk lorries actually widened the roads, which were built for a horse and cart," he recalls. Every scrap of cargo space was used: an extra top deck was built behind the cab to carry 12 churns and 6 more were carried on a tailboard. Hunt was 19 when the War ended but trucks were still hard to buy for the next five years.

Most manufacturers were using pre-War designs and many operators got hold of ex-army vehicles. The Co-op's faithful 5LWs were eventually replaced with bigger ERF tankers, and these in turn were succeeded by ERF eight-leggers powered by 150 and 180 Gardner engines, and then by E10s. Today the Co-op's milk division at Manchester runs about 90 E14s with 25,000-litre semi-trailer tankers. Based at five depots, they deliver to Co-op-owned and other creameries, all of which are controlled by the Milk Marketing Board (now Milk Marque). One of these, Cricklade Creameries in Swindon, has 9 ERFs among its 13 artics. The milk division also operates 107 17-tonne and 24-tonne tankers, about 20% of which are ERFs, on its milk collection runs to farms.

According to the division's group transport manager Sid Cartwright, who has been with the Co-op for 30 years, ERF's policy has changed little since the 1940s. "They still use the same system to build a vehicle to your specifications, and the cab still has a long life." The Co-op also runs ERFs on its supermarket dry goods distribution operation. Although it has used a lot of Iveco Fords and Renaults in the past few years, it is moving more to ERFs, says vehicle product manager Peter Fallon. Now about half its fleet comprises E6s and E10s. An ES6 17-tonner has been touring three of its 19 depots; Swindon and Bristol look likely to place orders. At its all-artic Newton Heath depot in Manchester, about 90% of its 60 vehicles are ERFs. Few people realize that the organization is one of the biggest retailers in Britain and that the Co-op's unique structure, with a network of local co-operative retail societies, means power comes from the bottom, not the top, says Fallon. The central Co-operative Wholesale Societies are contracted like any other third party supplier, and "if our price doesn't suit them they go elsewhere", he says.

1960s

As Britain emerged from the post-War austerity of the fifties, the sixties appeared as a truly brave new world - the "swinging" world of The Beatles, miniskirts, motorways, flower power, political scandal, irreverent satire and, of course, that 1966 football World Cup victory.

If the 1950s were years of consolidation for ERF, the sixties were years of rapid technical advance and innovation (not least as a result of legislative changes). But the decade began under a cloud with the death in October 1960 of Dennis Foden, who had been managing director since ERF's inception in 1933. A month later Peter Foden, then only 30 years old, took over the daunting job of leading the company. As he would recall much later. "There seemed to be a vacant chair and nobody about to fill it". ERF had earned steady profits during the late fifties but had the potential to do much better. Peter Foden set about bringing in a programme of changes to realize that potential sooner rather than later.

On the product front the company continued to push forward. In 1961 it launched one of the first "environmentally sensitive" heavy trucks - the 88.R eight-wheel rigid with rubber suspension and, at a time when diesel power units predominated in heavy CVs, a quieter Rolls Royce petrol engine. It won orders from the likes of Shell BP, delivering to hospitals and the Houses of Parliament, where minimum noise intrusion was paramount. While the old KV cab had clearly been successful, a replacement was well underway by the early sixties, again using the talents of designer Gerald Broadbent, who had worked on the original KV design at Jennings. The result of his work was the stylish, curving LV cab, based again on glass fibre external panelling, which bowed in a the 1962 Earls Court Motor Show. A year later *Commercial Motor* was describing the LV as "having the best appearance of any cab currently being offered on

British heavy vehicles, while its interior puts it well into the Continental 'luxury' classes".

If 1963 was a good year for ERF, with annual production reaching some 800 vehicles, it was less favourable to road haulage's traditional rival, the railways, with the publication of the controversial Beeching Report. The railways' loss was quickly transformed to the road hauliers' gain, with subsequent benefits for the truck makers. Another legislative change that was to have a major impact on the Sandbach-based company was the 1964 Construction and Use Regulations, which permitted the use of 32-tonne gross-weight articulated vehicles. ERF had long been expecting the change and was quick to capitalize on it. That same year Cummins engines were noticeably featured in ERF trucks at the Motor Show, demonstrating the company's intention to extend the choice of power units in its vehicles beyond the legendary Gardner.

ERF's growing domestic success was matched by an increasing export trade, with trucks being sent to places as far afield as Africa, Australia and New Zealand. While hauliers were still smarting from a 50% increase in road tax, in 1965 ERF remained committed to technical improvement. During a tour of the United States, chief engineer Ernest Sherratt was sufficiently impressed by the "fail-safe" spring brake concept developed by American engineering company MGM to try it out for himself. ERF approached the Ministry of Transport for permission to evaluate 50 sets of the spring brakes. The Ministry allowed the test, which eventually led to the adoption of spring bakes as standard on virtually every heavy truck sold in the UK. If hauliers were impressed by what ERF had to offer, the notoriously hard-to-please stock market was also "quite pleased with what it got," according to a contemporary report, when pre-tax profits rose to £345,911 on turnover up 30% to £4 million.

The desire to build ever better trucks spurred further product changes, including the use of the Fuller Roadranger twin-countershaft gearbox, which would soon become the standard gearbox on a large number of UK-built heavy trucks. After the launch of a new 16-tonner cab at Earls Court in 1968, along with a three-axle tractive unit with air suspension, ERF displayed two new export models with steel cabs at the Brussels Show in 1969 - the first time it had taken part in a Continental exhibition. But the proliferation of new models was not allowed to get out of hand.

Shortly before his retirement in 1969 Ernest Sherratt, interviewed by *Commercial Motor*, reinforced that fact: "It is possible to provide an optimum specification and yet retain a valuable degree of standardization. This is a difficult exercise, but it can be done. To the operator the right specification can mean all the difference between profit and loss. Getting it right is our business."

1970s

Without clear guidelines it was, as a contemporary editorial put it, a case of "designing in the dark", but that didn't dissuade ERF, which had a prototype 44-tonne tractive unit ready in time for the Scottish Motor Show in October 1969. Following a hysterical anti-juggernaut campaign, however, the idea of a 44-tonne UK truck limit would not be mooted again in this decade, but this setback did no harm to ERF's fortunes and in July 1970 it released figures for the financial year up to March 1970 which showed record-breaking pretax profits and sales of £734,700 and £9.7 million respectively. Possibly those figures encouraged the start of the sometimes bizarre on/off battle by ERF to buy Atkinson Lorries. After a series of bids from ERF, and counterbids from Sandbach-based rival Fodens, Atkinson finally merged with Seddon of Oldham. Seddon Atkinson was in turn acquired by International Harvester and finally bought by the Spanish company Enasa.

The biggest news of 1970, however, was not the battle for the big "A", but the Earls Court Motor Show debut of the ERF A-Series. Despite its obvious visual similarities to the old LV, the A-Series was much more than a cosmetic project. Beneath its cab major innovations included standard power steering, longer springs and bigger dampers which gave a better ride and handling. Weight had also been saved in the redesigned frame, but without compromising strength. Power was provided by the latest Cummins and Gardner engines, including the 240hp Gardner 8LXB. After a short demonstration spin at the show, *Commercial Motor* declared it "a very easy vehicle to drive with excellent brakes".

Following its savaging over the 44-tonne issue at the hands of the press, the road haulage industry received welcome support from Transport Minister John Peyton. At the official opening of ERF's new £1 million-plus Middlewich service centre in November 1971, he insisted that the heavy lorry was an enormous "benefactor" to the community. In 1972, long-awaited changes in Construction and Use Regulations finally allowed operators to run maximum-weight 32-tonne artics on four, rather than five axles. This helped to stimulate truck sales, although the first signs of a downturn in the economy were being noted by truck makers.

Although ERF remained staunchly convinced of the advantages offered by a glass fibre cab, in 1972 it extended its product range with a "British-spec" version of its all-steel export cab. A futuristic, all-steel cab also figured on ERF's striking "Eurotruck" heavy tractive unit, which broke cover at the Brussels Motor Show the following year. Throughout the 1950s and 1960s ERF had been at the forefront of commercial vehicle technology - particularly through its use of glass fibre cabs. But with the arrival of the B-Series it broke new ground with the adoption of "hot-pressed" plastic panels. Until 1974 ERF's method of cab production was long winded, with panels hand-laid in open moulds.

For the B-Series, however, they were produced by laying a coating of plastic resins over fibre glass, and these materials were then placed under pressure in a heated enclosed mould with a catalyst to form the finished panels. These were then attached to a strong steel subframe. The new SMC panels were dimensionally much more accurate than hand-produced components and were, of course, corrosion proof. The SP (steel/plastic) cab was clearly a major achievement in the development of composite materials and it would become the basis of the cab used on today's E-Series models.

By now the domination of Gardner engines in ERF trucks was being tested: by the middle seventies as many operators were choosing Cummins or Rolls Royce power units as those specifying Gardners. The mid-seventies also saw the disappearance of the David Brown gearbox as Fuller became the first transmission choice. The development of the B-Series, however, was not without its price. Together with a fall in heavy truck sales, and the growing impact of Continental competition, it would have a serious effect on the company's finances.

Despite strong South African sales and "encouraging results" from its new ERF Fire Engineering division, the company finished 1976 with a loss of £118,000. Self-appointed experts were quick to forecast its demise. ERF put the gloom merchants back in their place by bouncing back in 1977 with a £1.7 million profit.

By 1978 ERF was in an expansionist mood, and deciding to push cash spending having announced plans to complete a new assembly plant in Wrexham which would initially build the company's new M-Series middleweight rigids. The Welsh site was to be part of a £10 million capital expansion programme which already included the new Middlewich service centre. *In little more than a year, however, that optimism would be severely tested by the start of a calamitous recession with a severe impact on the company liquidity.*

1980-1982

To describe the recession of the early eighties as "serious" would be to indulge in the Great British habit for understatement - for the truck manufacturers it was catastrophic. In 1979 a total of 79,855 trucks and artics above 3.5 tonnes were registered in the UK. By 1982, the market had plummeted to 44,301, with the artic sector taking the worst hammering.

Case Study: ERF

1980-1982 Results

	1980 £000	1981 £000	1982 £000
Employment of Capital			
Tangible Assets	8,572	9,244	8,982
Investments	241	5	6
Current Assets less Liabilities	9,653	3,957	(701)
Total Shareholders Funds	18,466	13,206	8,287
Sales and Profits			
Sales to External Customers	82,126	55,752	52,345
Profit/(loss) before Taxation and extraordinary items	4,303	(4,219)	(3,272)
Taxation	171	132	208
Extraordinary Item	-	616	1,404
Profit/(loss) after Taxation and extraordinary items	4,132	(4,967)	(4,884)
Cost of Dividends	396	101	101
Total Retained Profits/(losses)	3,736	(5,068)	(4,985)
Financial Statistics			
Return on Capital	23.30	(31.95)	(39.48)
Gross Ordinary Dividend (pence)	6.00	0.14	0.14
Gross Ordinary Dividend (%)	24.00	0.57	0.57
Times Dividend Covered	13.34	-	-
Earnings/(loss) per share (pence)	53.79	(58.94)	(47.38)

Analysing this summary of results, we can see the severity of the downturn in performance - largely due to the recessional impact on this type of business sector and ERF's large exposure to the UK marketplace because they have few exports.

Shareholders' funds collapsed to £8.3 m from £18.5 m. Sales have dropped from £82.1 m to £52.3 m, with profits becoming losses of £4.9 m. Liquidity is under extreme pressure, with current liabilities exceeding current assets and bank indebtedness has mushroomed. Would ERF be able to survive?

Readers are encouraged to study the following extract from the 1982 accounts and in particular focus on the cash generative actions within the Chairman's statement and then go on to look closely at the Source and Application of Funds statement. **This** *shows that ERF have improved their cash flow within 1982 despite a negative entry point of £3272. This has been achieved by tighter management of cash flow within the working capital section. Notes 11, 12 and 13 give a fuller picture and readers will see little movement in stock; some deterioration in debtors but **the main cash flow change is in creditors** within one year – see note 13.*

Extract from 1982 Accounts:

Chairman's statement 1982

The net loss, before tax and extraordinary items, for the year ended 3rd April 1982 was £3.272m as compared with a net loss of £4.219m in 1981. The loss, after tax of £208,000 and extraordinary items of £1.404m was £4.884m (£4.967m in 1981). Group sales were £52.345m compared with £55.752m in 1981.

Redundancy charges included in the above figures were £516,000 (previous year £137,000). Both our South African and plastics subsidiaries reported good trading figures but, as reported in the interim accounts, it has been decided to close down our fire engineering subsidiary due to very difficult trading conditions and growing losses. This is reflected in the extraordinary item.

Whilst the group suffered another trading loss for the year, the second half gave some reason for optimism in that the trading loss before tax and interest was £318,000 compared with a trading loss of £1.576m in the first half.

Dividend proposals

In view of the group loss for 1981/82, the board recommend that only a nominal dividend of 0.1 per ordinary share be declared in order to preserve the trustee status of the company. No interim dividend has been paid.

Commercial vehicle operations

1982 continued to be a very difficult year with our UK trucks sales showing a reduction of 21% over 1981. However, export sales showed a considerable improvement and unit sales increased by over 50%, with export business now accounting for over a quarter of our total vehicle sales.

Our South African subsidiary sold a record 339 units and its turnover was up by 23% to over £10m. We have been successful in obtaining a sizable order from the Middle East during the trading year and we are hopeful that this new market for ERF will grow during the next twelve months.

The basic problem in the UK market can be entirely attributed to the continued economic stagnation in the UK and the strength of the pound relative to European currencies, which gives Common Market vehicle manufacturers a decided edge on price within the UK.

It is apparent that the heavy vehicle market sector has borne the brunt of the recession in the motor industry and there are still numbers of vehicles laid up or only partially utilized. In addition vehicle operators are being pressurized to keep rates at very low levels. All this, together with the Government's indecision on the heavy lorry, has kept demand at a continued low level.

However in the first quarter of 1982 there was a return to a higher level of activity, triggered off by special factors, including the rail strike and the anticipation of some improvement in UK economy. This, together with improved export business, put us back on to a five-day week, albeit at a reduced output.

Our product has continued to be developed and improved and we have been able to substantially reduce the unladen weight to give customers a higher payload.

We are also going ahead with designs for higher vehicle weights, as and when they are approved. A further reduction in manpower was unfortunately necessary to equate with reduced production levels. We are now operating at a much higher level of efficiency. During the first quarter of our new financial year we have managed to increase output further, although we are still well below our full capacity.

Our service division experienced a substantial upturn in parts sales in the latter half of the trading year as more and more vehicles were put back on the road and vehicle life has generally been extended.

A new computer facility was put into operation in April this year, which we believe will improve our efficiency in the parts division, and give the customer a better service and the company better control over parts inventory.

Other group activities

ERF Plastics has had another good year despite the disruptions caused by moving into a new factory. Its product range has been consistently expanded into new fields and there is an increasing demand for hot moulded plastics from a wide range of industries. The new pressing facilities now on stream will give the company a much greater capacity, which is being fully explored.

As reported in my interim statement, the board reluctantly decided to close down its CFE subsidiary due to mounting losses. Attempts were made to sell the company off as a going concern, and we did investigate the possibility of a management buy-out; unfortunately neither of these alternatives were considered to be viable.

The future

The second year of the recession has been and gone and we are now entering the third, with some guarded optimism. However, it is likely that a substantial recovery in the UK economy will not come quickly, and whilst we have experienced some increase in business we do not believe that there will be a notable improvement before the second half of our trading year, but with every possibility of a more marked improvement in 1983.

The fortunes of the commercial vehicle industry are closely tied to the economy, as we are basically a service industry. The demise of many independent truck companies means that we are the last of the independent truck companies in a world of multinationals. During severe trading conditions, price distortions are caused by over-production in a dwindling market and we are therefore reducing our operational costs where possible, and keeping our prices competitive, to hold our market share, but at the same time maintaining our quality and ensuring a first-class back-up service throughout our distributor organization.

We are now planning to offset the vagaries of the UK market by decreasing our dependence on the home market and finding overseas markets suitable for our type of product, however we do need a strong UK market to act as a firm base for our company's operation.

The plastics company is now entering a new phase and will, I am sure, contribute more to the group's income in future.

Board changes
Since the last AGM we have had three changes to the board which I must mention:

Firstly the resignation of our deputy chairman, Ernest Sherratt, who has been with the company since its inception in 1933, when he was appointed chief designer. Whilst he retired from executive position in June 1969, he has remained on the board and been actively engaged in a consultative capacity with us since then. His devotion to the company cannot be adequately expressed, but on behalf of the board and shareholders we thank him most sincerely.

The second change is the retirement, in April 1982, of Eric Green, who has been with the company for fifteen years in many capacities, and latterly as deputy chairman of the vehicle manufacturing operation. During his time with us he had a significant effect on the growth and success of the company.

Finally, Albert Wheway was appointed as a non-executive director in October 1981. His industry and banking experience are proving to be very helpful to the company at this crucial time.

Personnel
Another difficult year has meant more redundancies, right across the board, but hopefully as business improves we will be recruiting and anticipate re-engaging some of those who worked with us in the past. Wages and salaries have been held at levels enabling us to stay competitive and I must thank all those who supported us, especially in the areas of productivity where much has been achieved.

Finally I would like to thank all the employees for their continued support during the past year and hope that this time next year I will be able to report a much improved situation.

E P Foden
Chairman/Managing Director

18 June 1982

Results at a glance

	1982	1981	%Change
	£000	£000	
Sales to external customers	52,345	55,752	-6.1
Loss before taxation	(3,272)	(4,219)	+22.4
Shareholders funds	8,287	13,206	-37.2
Loss per ordinary share	(49.36)p	(61.41)p	+19.6
Return on capital employed	(39.1)%	(31.4)%	-24.5
Dividends			
Dividends per ordinary share	0.1p	0.1p	-

Case Study: ERF

Consolidated Profit and Loss Account
for the fifty-two weeks ended 3 April 1982

	Note	1982 £000	1982 £000	1981 £000	1981 £000
Turnover	1		52,345		55,752
External charges					
Increase in stocks of finished goods work in progress		1,305		3,526	
Own work capitalized		(347)		(83)	
Raw materials and consumables		(41,840)		(46,690)	
Other external charges		(4,287)	(45,169)	(4,844)	(48,091)
Staff costs	2		(8,439)		(9,685)
Depreciation			(631)		(652)
Interest payable	3		(1,378)		(1,543)
Loss on ordinary activities before taxation	1&4		(3,272)		(4,219)
Taxation on ordinary activities	5		(208)		(132)
Loss on ordinary activities after taxation			(3,480)		(4,351)
Extraordinary item	6		(1,404)		(616)
Loss for the financial year	7		(4,884)		(4,967)
Proposed dividend	8		(101)		(101)
Loss transferred to reserves			(4,985)		(5,068)
Loss per ordinary share	9		(49.36)p		(61.41)p
Loss per ordinary share fully diluted			(47.67)p		(59.29)p

Consolidated Balance Sheet
at 3 April 1982

	Note	1982 £000	1982 £000	1981 £000	1981 £000
Fixed assets	10		8,982		9,244
Current assets					
Stocks	11&12	16,059		16,180	
Debtors	11	6,739		5,266	
Investments		6		5	
Bank balance and cash in hand		9		104	
		22,813		21,555	
Creditors amounts falling due within one year	13	22,038		15,708	
Net current assets			775		5,847
Total assets less current liabilities			9,757		15,091
Creditors amounts falling due after one year	14		1,470		1,885
Net assets			8,287		13,206
Capital and reserves					
Share capital	15		2,745		2,744
Reserves			5,542		10,462
			8,287		13,206

E P Foden
J W Hobbs Directors

The accounts and notes were approved by the board of directors on 18 June 1982.

Case Study: ERF

Statement of Source and Application of Funds
for the fifty-two weeks ended 3 April 1982

	1982		1981	
	£000	£000	£000	£000
Loss before taxation and extraordinary item		(3,272)		(4,219)
Adjustments not involving movement of funds				
Depreciation (after adjustment for disposals)		630		642
Loss on investment		-		137
Funds absorbed by operations		(2,642)		(3,440)
Movements in working capital				
Decrease in stocks	121		6,574	
(Increase)/decrease in debtors	(1,473)		2,146	
Increase/(decrease) in creditors due within one year	6,470		(11,269)	
Resulting in a net source/(application) of		5,118		(2,549)
Purchase of fixed assets	(796)		(1,667)	
Extraordinary item (amount affecting funds movement)	(1,103)		(616)	
Proceeds from sale of fixed assets	196		335	
(Decrease)/increase in creditors due after one year	(415)		1,173	
		(2,118)		(775)
(Purchase)/sale of investments		(1)		99
Taxation paid		(200)		(174)
Dividend paid		(101)		(245)
Total source/(application) of funds		2,698		(3,644)
Increase/(decrease) in funds		56		(7,084)
Represented by				
Decrease/(increase) in bank borrowing		56		(7,084)

Notes to the accounts

1. Analysis of group trading results before taxation

	1982		1981	
	Sales	Profit/(Loss)	Sales	Profit/(Loss)
	£000	£000	£000	£000
Commercial vehicles	48,176	(3,186)	48,204	(4,446)
Fire appliances	2,283	(281)	6,325	(18)
Other	1,886	195	1,223	245
	52,345	(3,272)	55,752	(4,219)

Geographical analysis	%	%	%	%
UK based operations				
Home trade	70.9		78.1	
Europe	0.2		0.7	
New Zealand	0.1	(112.6)	0.5	(107.0)
Middle East	3.6		0.9	
Others	4.5		4.0	
South African based operations	20.7	12.6	15.8	7.0
	100.0	(100.0)	100.0	(100.0)

2. Staff numbers and cost

The average number of personnel employed by the company, including full-time executive directors, during the year was as follows:

	1982	1981
Management	108	113
Administration	328	445
Production and sales	870	1,132
	1,306	1,690

Case Study: ERF

The aggregate payroll costs were	£000	£000
Wages and salaries	7,166	8,376
Social security costs	521	571
Other pension costs	752	738
	8,439	9,685

3. Interest

	1982	1981
	£000	£000
Interest on bank overdraft	991	1,282
Interest on unsecured loan stock	9	11
Interest on medium term bank loan	22	57
Interest received on short-term deposits and loans	(16)	(39)
	1,006	1,311
Interest on export finance (net)	372	232
	1,378	1,543

4. Loss on ordinary activities

The following amounts have been charged

Directors' emoluments		
Chairman and highest paid director		
(£19,000 after tax)	32	37
Other directors (analysed below)	79	101
Contribution to pension schemes	35	34
Short-time working subsidy	(3)	(4)
Compensation for loss of office	28	-
	171	168

Hire of plant, equipment and motor vehicles	187	257
Auditors' remuneration (overseas £10,500)	30	35
Redundancy costs	516	137
Loss on investment	-	137
Exchange losses/(profits)(including translation differences)	64	(115)

The following amounts have been credited

Short time working subsidy	309	1,074
Profit on sale of fixed assets	18	7
Income from investments	1	13

Analysis of other directors' emoluments

£	1982	1981
0- 5,000	3	2
5001- 10,000	1	-
20,001- 25,000	3	3
25,001- 30,000	-	1

5. Taxation

	1982	1981
	£000	£000
United Kingdom		
Corporation tax	-	-
Advance corporation tax not immediately recoverable	43	43
Overseas		
Taxation on profits for the year	165	89
	208	132

Case Study: ERF

6. Extraordinary item

The extraordinary item provides for the costs of closure of Cheshire Fire Engineering Limited. In 1981, it related to irrecoverable expenditure on the company's planned expansion project at Wrexham which was discontinued.

7. Loss for the financial year

Parent company - excluding subsidiary company dividends	(163)	(160)
Subsidiaries	(4,721)	(4,807)
	(4,884)	(4,967)

8. Dividends

	1982	1981
	£000	£000
Ordinary dividends		
Interim	-	-
Proposed final 0.1p per ordinary share	7	7
	7	7
Preference dividends	94	94
	101	101

The dividend of 0.1 pence on the ordinary shares is the minimum necessary to preserve the trustee status of the company.

9. Loss per ordinary share

(a) Loss per ordinary share has been calculated on the loss after tax and preference dividend, but before extraordinary item, of £3,574,000 (1981 loss £4,445,000) and on 7,239,769 ordinary shares in issue (1981 7,237,884).

(b) Fully diluted loss per ordinary share has been calculated on the same basis but before charging interest on the convertible loan stock, and allowing for the maximum number of shares into which the loan stock is convertible in 1982 i.e. 238,924 giving a total number of ordinary shares of 7,478,693 (1981 7,478,693).

10. Fixed assets

	Total	Free hold land and buildings	Short term leasehold buildings	Plant	Leased equipment	Office equipment	Motor vehicles
	£000	£000	£000	£000	£000	£000	£000
Cost of valuation at 4 April 1981	10,652	5,367	29	4,267	249	212	528
Adjustment for currency translations	(36)	(28)	-	(3)	-	(2)	(3)
Additions	796	37	(5)	266	-	44	454
Assets written off	(273)	-	(24)	(217)	-	(21)	(11)
	11,139	5,376	-	4,313	249	233	968
Less disposals	(267)	(16)	-	(13)	-	(4)	(234)
At 3 April 1992							
Cost	3,527	556	-	1,854	249	134	734
Valuation	7,345	4,804	-	2,446	-	95	-
	10,872	5,360	-	4,300	249	229	734
Depreciation at 4 April 1981	1,408	88	6	984	35	43	252
Charge for the year	648	92	5	385	36	41	89
Adjustments for currency translations	(3)	-	-	(1)	-	(1)	(1)
	2,053	180	11	1,368	71	83	340
Less disposals	(89)	-	-	(1)	-	(2)	(86)
Assets written off	(74)	-	(11)	(51)	-	(6)	(6)
	1,890	180	-	1,316	71	75	248

Net book values at
4 April 1981	9,244	5,279	23	3,283	214	169	276
3 April 1982	8,982	5,180	-	2,984	178	154	486

Fixed assets with the exception of product tooling and motor vehicles were revalued at 29 March 1980 at open market value on the basis of existing use.

11. Debtors

	1982 £000	1981 £000
Trade debtors	6,136	4,688
Other debtors	462	457
Prepayments	141	121
	6,739	5,266

Export Credits Guarantee Department hold a notarial bond for £4,095,000 (1981 £3,950,000) which may give rise to charge on the stocks and debtors of the South African subsidiary.

12. Stocks

	1982 £000	1981 £000
Finished goods	3,600	3,305
Work in progress	4,886	3,693
Production materials and components	3,417	5,407
Service parts for resale	4,488	4,885
	16,391	17,290
Less progress payments receivable	332	1,110
	16,059	16,180

Goods to the value of £762,000 (1981 Nil) in respect of which suppliers hold retention are included in the stock value. These goods were supplied against a large export contract.

13 Creditors amounts falling due within one year

Group

Bank loans and overdrafts	6,997	7,148
Trade creditors	9,631	4,334
Bills payable	2,940	2,000
Taxation	116	105
Deposits on account	213	145
Dividends	46	46
Other creditors	2,095	1,930
	22,038	15,708

Parent company

Taxation	20	20
Dividends	46	46
Bank loans and overdrafts	-	92
Other creditors	877	673
	943	831

The UK bank borrowings from Barclays Bank plc are secured by means of a debenture given by member companies of the group constituting a fixed charge on UK properties and debts and floating charge on the remaining UK assets of the group. There is also a cross guarantee whereby each UK member company undertakes joint and several liability in respect of the total amount outstanding which at 3 April 1982 was £6,937,000.

14. Creditors amounts falling due after one year

	1982 £000	1981 £000
Bills payable	1,108	1,470
Loan capital (parent company)	134	135
Mortgage loan	107	113
Leasing commitments	121	167
	1,470	1,885

a) The bills payable are due for payment over a period of up to two years from the balance sheet date.

b) The 8% convertible unsecured loan stock 1988/93 may be converted into ordinary shares of E.R.F. (Holdings) plc up to 31 March, 1993. The present conversion terms are 178.3443 ordinary shares for every £100 of stock. During the year holders of £1,057 loan stock have exercised their option.

c) The mortgage loan is secured by a mortgage bond over the overseas property to which it relates. The loan is repayable in full in March 1984.

d) Leasing commitments are due for payment up to four years from the balance sheet date.

15. Share capital

a) Authorized

1,500,000 10% cumulative preference shares of £1 each	1,500	1,500
10,000,000 ordinary shares of 25p each	2,500	2,500
	4,000	4,000

b) Issued

934,837 10% cumulative preference shares of £1 each	935	935
7,239,769 ordinary shares of 25p each	1,810	1,809
	2,745	2,744

Number of ordinary shares in issue increased by 1,885 to holders of £1,057 8% convertible loan stock 1988/93.

Part 2 - Actions taken by ERF

As ERF's managing director Cyril Acton would later recall: "By May 1980 it just collapsed on us. At the end of 1979 we were building 16 trucks a day. In the depth of the recession it was 16 a week - the bottom just fell out of the market." Ironically, at the start of 1980 things were still looking fairly rosy for ERF. In January it announced that it had been offered a £5 million loan by the European Coal and Steel Community to finance its expansion programme, including an assembly plant at Wrexham. By September of that year, it was making "further redundancies" among its Sandbach workforce, which would eventually be trimmed from 1,400 to just over 600 by the end of 1983, with the factory on a two-day week.

Not all was gloom and doom, however. The following month ERF revealed a trio of new "Weightsaver" models in time for the Birmingham Motor Show, comprising a Rolls-Royce-powered tractor and a six and eight-wheeler. Speaking at the Show, Chairman Peter Foden warned operators of the dangers of falling standards, particularly on maintenance, as the haulage business tore itself apart with desperate rate cutting. At the same show the news broke that ERF's Sandbach neighbours, Foden, had been bought by the American truck builder Paccar.

Despite the strong competition for work, 1980 would hold some joy for hauliers. After 15 months of deliberation, the Armitage Report on Lorries, People and the Environment recommended a maximum 44-tonne limit for articulated trucks on six axles. But it was to be some two years before Transport Minister David Howell bit the bullet and pushed through watered-down legislation allowing 38-tonners. The start of 1981 was marked by two black spots. On 10 January ERF reported that because of the depressed state of the UK truck market, and the "withholding" of financial support from the Department of Industry, plans for the Wrexham assembly plant would have to be abandoned and its Fire Engineering division put up for sale.

There was still plenty of interest in the new C36 Trailblazer tractive unit when it debuted at the Scottish Motor Show, complete with a Spicer gearbox in place of a Fuller. But a more radical vehicle appeared a year later at the Birmingham show in the shape of the "Project QM" middleweight chassis with full air suspension and an unusual rear axle located by a large A-frame.

1983 was anything but a dull year for ERF. In June the question on everybody's lips was: "Who's buying ERF shares?", following a report in the Mail on Sunday - quickly denied - that the Dutch truck maker Daf had been buying them. Whether there really was a mystery buyer or not, the share price certainly went up. The biggest story of the year, however, had yet to come. Following months of press speculation, ERF confirmed that it had agreed in principle with the Japanese truck maker Hino to assemble a range of 12-15-tonne middleweight trucks at its Sandbach plant, using Hino chassis, cabs and axles with British engines. "Production starts in time for a launch early next year" *Commercial Motor* confidently reported in July. Then exchange rates, the traditional stumbling block of international deals, came into play: an unfavourable change in the value of the yen killed the agreement stone dead before it got off the ground.

Nonetheless ERF remained firmly committed to the middleweight market. In autumn 1983 it unveiled its own M16 16-tonner complete with a revised C-Series cab, and as ERF began looking at the opportunities beyond its traditional heavy truck home ground, it began making a number of significant changes to the way it sold its products.

Most of ERF's sales and marketing activities had previously been carried out by its dealers and distributors, but in 1983 it set up its own marketing and sales force. In parallel with this the company decided to further rationalize its product range, concentrating on building its trucks using the most suitable components. The result was the CP (Common Parts) Series, launched the following year with a no-nonsense Cummins engine/Eaton gearbox/Rockwell axle combination which would prove highly popular with hauliers.

By June 1985, Peter Foden was confidently reporting that ERF was back on the road to profitability, with a new range on the way. A year later his prediction was proved correct. By January ERF had bounced back into the black with a £1.3 million pre-tax profit, and less than four months later the E-Series tractor debuted with a more aerodynamic, squared-off, SP4 cab complete with an all new interior, marketed as a "New refinement in pedigree." As truck buyers came flocking back over the next two years ERF was well placed to take advantage of the new business, with a modern range and production line churning out 17 trucks a day by early 1988. By the end of the year it was 21 a day. With the return of the sales came better earnings, and pre-tax profits for 1987 rose from £718,000 to a cool £5.61 million. By the end of 1988 ERF had also registered 3,740 trucks in the UK to win 10% of the market above 16 tonnes.

The next big news from ERF in 1988 was the signing of an agreement with the Austrian truck maker Steyr, under which ERF would use the all-steel Steyr cab on its attractive new ES6 17-tonner (launched at the 1988 Motor Show, along with ERF's new range of E8 light tractors and multi-wheelers), while Steyr would receive plastic components from ERF in return. The new ES6 and E8 trucks would remain loyal to the Cummins/Eaton/Rockwell team.

Group Results for the Last Ten Years

	Note	1986 £000	1987 £000	1988 £000	1989 £000	1990 £000	1991 £000	1992 £000	1993 £000	1994 £000	1995 £000
Employment of capital											
Tangible assets	3	8,512	8,444	12,018	13,005	14,240	13,238	17,282	18,917	19,847	19,532
Investments		7	8	8	9	100	33	-	-	72	267
Current assets less liabilities		(236)	517	4,933	14,608	14,768	15,109	11,372	5,165	3,329	3,547
Net assets employed		8,283	8,969	16,959	27,622	29,108	28,380	28,654	24,082	23,248	23,346
Sales and profits											
Sales to external customers		71,028	75,911	121,919	164,492	148,001	102,548	117,887	111,709	149,500	202,369
Profit/(loss) before taxation		1,272	718	5,606	7,842	3,270	(2,464)	(613)	(4,123)	(26)	2,281
Tax charge/(credit)		-	-	431	2,298	984	(406)	469	254	282	366
Minority interests		-	-	-	-	-	(178)	(124)	(60)	(87)	(181)
Profit/(loss) after taxation attributable to the ERF Group		1,272	718	5,175	5,544	2,286	(2,236)	(1,206)	(4,437)	(395)	1,734
Cost of dividends		-	-	773	1,460	1,065	583	485	289	289	534
Total retained profits/(losses)		1,272	718	4,402	4,084	1,221	(2,819)	(1,691)	(4,726)	(684)	1,200
Financial statistics											
Return on capital (%)	1	15.36	8.01	33.06	28.39	11.23	(8.68)	(2.14)	(17.12)	(0.11)	9.77
Net ordinary dividend (pence)		-	-	9.00	15.00	10.00	5.00	4.00	2.00	2.00	4.50
Net ordinary dividend (%)		-	-	36.00	60.00	40.00	20.00	16.00	8.00	8.00	18.00
Times dividend covered	2	-	-	7.38	3.99	2.26	-	-	-	-	3.72
Earnings/(loss) per share (pence)	4	15.63	8.26	65.42	66.48	22.65	(23.86)	(13.26)	(46.25)	(4.98)	16.75
Net debt to equity (%)	5	158	131	69	N/A	29	6	17	36	64	56

Notes

1. The return on capital is profit/(loss), before taxation, as a percentage of net assets employed.
2. Dividend cover represents profit attributable to the ERF Group after taxation and preference dividends divided by the total ordinary dividends declared.
3. Included in fixed assets are revaluation surpluses of £2.783m (in 1980); £0.627m (in 1984); £3.770m (in 1988); £0.144m (in 1989); £0.052m (in 1990) and £2.07m (in 1992).
4. The earnings/(loss) per ordinary share figures for the years up to and including 1988 have been restated to account for the 1989 rights issue at less than full market value. The figures for the years up to 1992 have been restated for the effects of reclassification arising from the adoption of Financial Reporting Standard No. 3 except insofar as they relate to the results of discontinued activities.
5. Net debt to equity represents the ratio of interest bearing borrowings less cash balances, (including deposits received in advance), to total net assets employed and has been restated for the effects arising from the adoption of Financial Reporting Standard No. 5.

Readers will see that this chart indicates the gradual recovery of ERF from the bleak 1982 position with sales progressing and peaking in 1989 at £164m. with a resultant profit of £7.8m. Cash flow has been improving and a glance at the net debt to equity ratio will reveal an ungeared position in 1989 before ERF enter the next recession. As we have seen before, due to the dramatic effect of cyclical downturns on this type of business, sales begin to plummet and losses are incurred, *resulting again in cash flow pressures*. Sales recover in 1994 but with only a breakeven position.

In the year 1995 sales reach an all-time record of £202m but profits are modest relative to turnover at £2.2m. The consolidated balance sheet as at 1st April 1995 shows a net worth of £23.3m and the consolidated cash-flow statement shows a cash positive inflow of £4.8m (prepared under the FRS 1 format).

Consolidated Balance Sheet
at 1 April, 1995

	Note	1995 £000	1995 £000	1994 £000	1994 £000
Fixed assets					
Tangible assets	13		19,532		19,847
Investment in associated undertaking	20		267		72
			19,799		19,919
Current assets					
Stocks	11	34,765		29,202	
Debtors	12	32,085		22,874	
Security deposits	15	-		819	
Cash at bank and in hand		4,091		100	
		70,941		52,995	
Creditors - amounts falling due within one year	14	(56,160)		(42,889)	
Net current assets			14,781		10,106
Total assets less current liabilities			34,580		30,025
Creditors - amounts falling due after more than one year	15		(6,334)		(2,621)
Provisions for liabilities and charges	16		(4,900)		(4,156)
Net assets			23,346		23,248
Capital and reserves					
Called up share capital	18		3,385		3,384
Share premium account	19		6,593		6,590
Revaluation reserve	19		6,180		6,566
Other capital reserves	19		835		1,043
Profit and loss account	19		4,234		3,460
Shareholders' funds - equity			20,292		20,108
- non-equity			935		935
			21,227		21,043
Minority interest - all equity			2,119		2,205
			23,346		23,248

Consolidated Cash Flow Statement
for the fifty-two weeks ended 1 April, 1995

	Note	1995 £000	1995 £000	1994 £000	1994 £000
Net cash flow from operating activities	26		9,645		2,318
Returns on investments and servicing of finance					
Interest received		70		162	
Interest paid		(1,362)		(1,459)	
Interest element of finance lease payments		(400)		(358)	
Dividends paid		(485)		(289)	
Dividends paid to minority interests		(43)		(31)	
Net cash outflow from returns on investments and servicing of finance			(2,220)		(1,975)
Taxation					
UK corporation tax (paid)/received		(80)		69	
Overseas tax paid		(222)		(173)	
Tax paid			(302)		(104)
Investing activities					
Purchase of tangible fixed assets		(2,368)		(4,119)	
Sale of tangible fixed assets		120		68	
Acquisition of subsidiary undertaking	31	(71)		-	
Net cash flow from investing activities			(2,319)		(4,051)
Net cash inflow/(outflow) before financing			4,804		(3,812)
Financing					
Issue of ordinary share capital	18	(4)		(2)	
Repayment of mortgage loans		33		146	
Inception of term loan	29	(4,000)		-	
Capital element of finance lease rental payments	29	1,372		1,114	
Finance leases entered into during the period	29	(1,354)		(2,411)	
Net cash inflow from financing			(3,953)		(1,153)
Increase/(decrease) in cash and cash equivalents	28		8,757		(2,659)
			4,804		(3,812)

> **Extract from Chairman's Letter to ERF Shareholders:**
> To ERF shareholders and, for information only, to participants in the ERF Share Option Schemes.
>
> **Recommended cash ordinary share offer and a preference share offer by Western Star for ERF.**
>
> **Background to and reasons for the offers**
> ERF's principal market has been the United Kingdom in which we compete with major European truck manufacturers such as Scania, Volvo, Iveco and Mercedes. As a result of this competition, we have suffered pressure on margins and on our share of the United Kingdom market. We have historically had a presence in South Africa and in a number of other export markets and have recently commenced marketing vehicles in France and Spain.
>
> The Board has for some time been considering the alternatives available to ERF to increase our export sales and reduce our dependence on the highly competitive United Kingdom market. On April 4 1996, we announced that we had enterred into discussions with Western Star to assess the potential of joint marketing opportunities for our complementary vehicles ranges, particularly in export markets.
>
> During the course of these discussions, we and Western Star concluded that significant benefits could be achieved through the merger of the two businesses. ERF has a strong brand name in the United Kingdom, and provides an entry point into the European and African markets, where Western Star does not currently have a presence. There are also opportunities to extend the marketing of ERF's "cab-over" format truck product range through Western Star's international distribution network, particularly in Australia.
>
> The combined entity will also have the scope to realize potential benefits in relation to engineering, research and development and materials purchasing. Accordingly, your board has agreed to recommend the merger of the businesses.

Part 3 - ERF PLC - Valuation

First we need to evaluate the offer by Western Star to identify the value it places on the equity and business of ERF. Then we need to consider the value of ERF from the viewpoint of the company. To do this we shall consider the market value, the value of the anticipated future cash flows and the asset value of the business. Then we shall compare these alternative valuation measures with the accounting data. Finally we shall examine the valuation logic being used by

Case Study: ERF

Western Star to assess whether the buyer sees added value in ERF which may not be readily apparent.

Evaluation of the Western Star Trucks offer
Western Star have offered the following:-

    For each ERF ordinary share   275p in cash
    For each ERF preference share 120p in cash

The 1 April 1995 accounts of ERF reveal the number of shares in issue as:-

    Ordinary shares   9,799,347
    Preference shares   934,837

The total value of the offer for the whole of the equity of ERF Limited is therefore:-

    Ordinary shares   £26,948,204
    Preference shares   £1,121,804
    Total value of the offer £28,030,000

Comparison with market values
The share price history, taken from appendix 5 of the offer document. is as follows:-

	ERF	
Ordinary shares		
Preference shares		
1 November 1995	281	100
1 December 1995	274	100
2 January 1996	251	100
1 February 1996	182xd	100
1 March 1996	189	98
1 April 1996	178	98xd
1 May 1996	233	109
16 May 1996	243	109
17 May 1996	273	109

The offer is an agreed offer. This means that discussions and negotiations had been going on between ERF and Western Star for some time prior to the bid.

Secondly, the offer is very close in value to the price of the shares just prior to the offer being made public, the market value of the ERF equity being £27,771,189 and the offer representing a 1% premium over the market price just prior to announcing the offer. So, there is no significant premium being offered here for control.

Valuation on a cash flow basis

A useful model showing the concept of cash-flow valuation is illustrated below. In general terms a company can be valued by forecasting future cash flows, including a terminal value and then discounting values at the average cost of capital to arrive at a net value of the equity

The historic cash flows of ERF are shown overleaf in abbreviated format:

Case Study: ERF

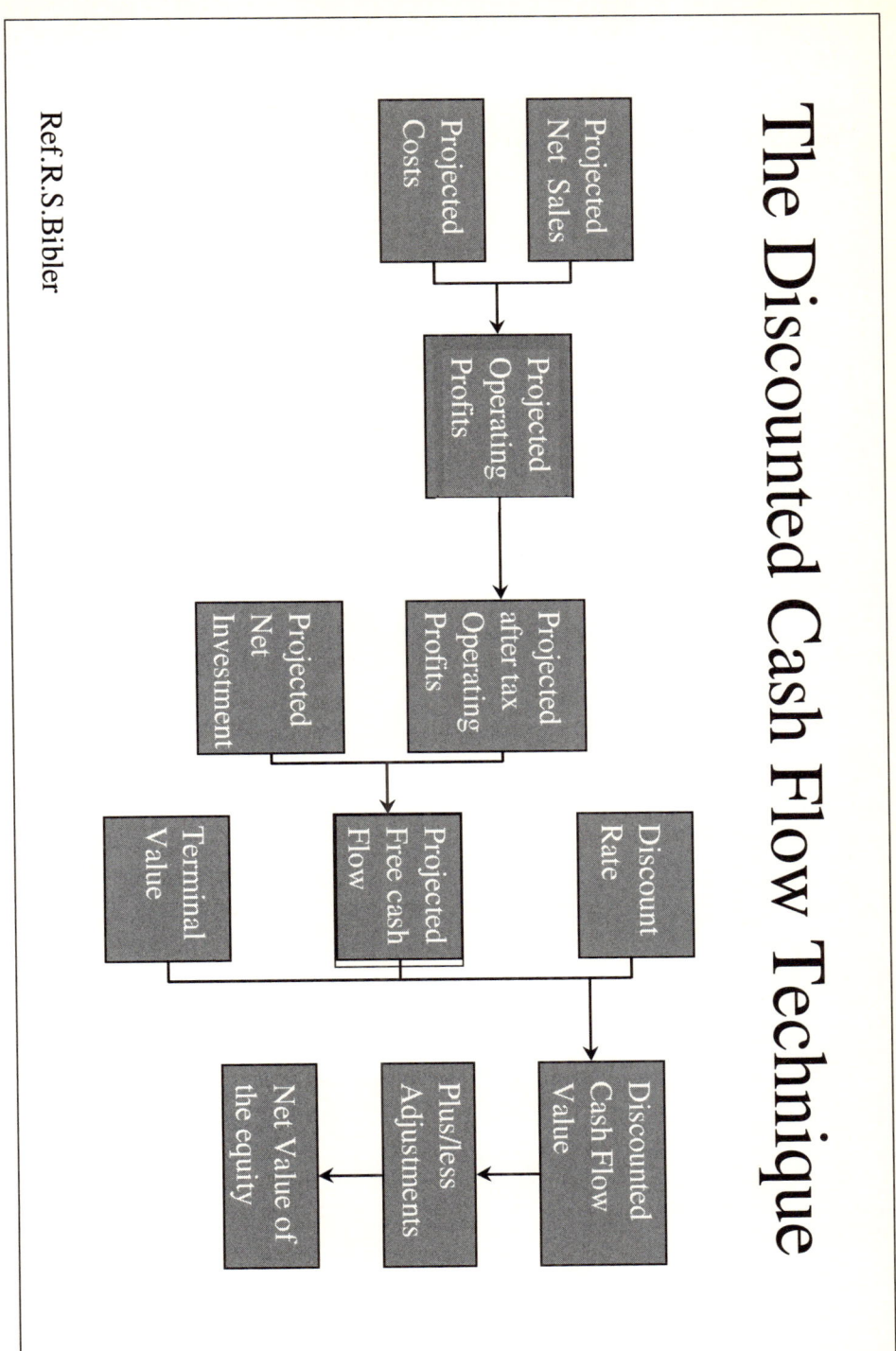

The Discounted Cash Flow Technique

Ref.R.S.Bibler

Discounted Cash Flow Valuation of a Company ($ thousands)

	1987	1988	1989	1990	1991	Terminal Value
Sales	34,800	45,000	50,850	57,461	64,930	
Gross Margin	6,720	7,875	8,899	10,056	11,362	
SG&A	3,456	4,050	4,577	5,172	5,843	
Operating Income	3,264	3,825	4,322	4,884	5,519	
Taxes	1,306	1,301	1,469	1,661	1,876	
Net Operating Income	1,958	2,524	2,853	3,223	3,643	9x
						32,787
Capital Requirements:						
Working Capital	(505)	(831)	(268)	(304)	(344)	
Fixed Assets (Net Dep)	134	(1,775)	(2,027)	(2,000)	(2,000)	
Free Cash Flow	1,587	(82)	558	919	1,299	
Net Present Value at 12%	1,417	(65)	397	584	737	18,604

Sum of Present Values 21,674
Less: Market Value of Debt 13,348
Estimated Value 8,326

ERF plc

Summary of cash flow data	1995	1994	1993	1992	1991
Operating cash flow	6874	4421	-1211	1834	-2210
Movement in net working assets	2771	-2103	3090	-1159	7568
Net capital expenditure	-2319	-4051	-2468	-3628	2988
Taxation	-302	-104	191	-651	-1369
Free cash flow	7024	-1837	-398	-3604	6977
Interest paid	-1692	-1655	-832	-319	-372
Dividends paid	-528	-320	-333	-646	-872
Cash generated (absorbed)	4804	-3812	-1563	-4569	5733
New equity	-4	-2	-2	0	-100
Movement on debt	-3949	-1151	2114	-1492	2994
Decrease/(Increase) in cash & equivalents	8757	-2659	-3675	-3077	2839
Total Funding	4804	-3812	-1563	-4569	5733

ERF plc
Free Cash Flow

All year-ends to 1 April	1995	1994	1993	1992	1991
Effective tax rate	0.33	0.33	0.33	0.3325	0.33
Operating cash flow	6874	4421	-1211	1834	-2210
Movement in net working assets	2771	-2103	3090	-1159	7568
Net capital expenditure	-2319	-4051	-2468	-3628	2988
Ungeared tax charge	-861	-651	-84	-758	-1492
Ungeared free cash flow	6465	-2384	-673	-3711	6854

ERF plc
Free Cash Flow Adjusted for Acquisitions and Disposals

All year-ends to 1 April	1995	1994	1993	1992	1991
Operating cash flow	6874	4421	-1211	1834	-2210
Movement in net working assets	2771	-2103	3090	-1159	7568
Net capital expenditure	-2248	-4051	-2648	-3628	-2138
Taxation	-861	-651	-84	-758	-1492
Ungeared Operating Free Cash Flow	6536	-2384	-673	-3711	1728

As we can see from the summary, ERF has only produced a positive free cash flow in two out of the five years, 1991 and 1995. In 1992, 1993 and 1994 the business has negative ungeared free cash flows. The summation of the five years is 1496 positive.

Forecasting the future cash flows of ERF

The next table offers an estimated forecast of the possible future free cash flows of ERF.

Free cash flow adjusted for acquisitions and disposals

All year-ends to 1 April	1996	1997	1998	1999	2000	2001	2002	2003	2004	2005
	1	2	3	4	54	6	7	8	9	10
Operating cash flow	7000	4000	-2000	2000	3000	6000	1000	2000	5000	7000
Movement in net working assets	1000	1000	1000	-500	-1000	-2000	2000	-500	-500	-500
Net capital expenditure	-2500	-2500	-2000	-1500	-2500	-3000	-3500	-3000	-3000	-3000
Taxation	-2000	-2000	-500	0	-500	-1000	-2000	0	-500	-1500
Ungeared operating free cash flow	3500	500	-3500	0	-1000	0	-2500	-1500	1000	2000
Discounted cash flows at cost of capital 10.3%	3173	411	-2608	0	-613	0	-1259	-685	414	750
Sum of the discounted cash flows Yrs 1 to 10	-416									

The forecast of future free cash flows has been prepared to the nearest £500,000. It offers a very broad approximation of what the cash flows might look like over the next ten years if the company continues with its existing strategies. The purpose of this example is to illustrate that, assuming the operating cash flow continues in a cyclical pattern as it has done in the past and the company has to continue to invest in fixed and working capital at similar rates to that experienced in the past then the business is unlikely to generate much positive free cash flow.

On the basis of the values chosen the 10-year discounted cash flow value is *negative*. This method of valuation of a company in ERF's case is not appropriate due to the volatility of cash flows and therefore a calculation of the terminal value has not been attempted.

Comparison of book values to the value of the offer and the market value of equity

The book value of equity in the last published balance sheet was £23.3m; the offer for the equity has a value of £28m. The premium over the book value is therefore only £4.7m.

The conclusion from the differing analysis methods show that it is better to consider the transaction as an asset-based value plus a small premium deal rather than a deal driven by expected future cash flows. We can only presume that the bid is attractive to the ERF board because the management of Western Star have stated their intention to allow ERF to continue to operate autonomously and both parties see benefits in the complementary nature of the merged group's world coverage. Despite not having a significant value from a projected cash flow point of view ERF enjoys a brand and geographic coverage which is valuable to other competitors. The alternative for any new company of setting up and developing a new brand is likely to require far more cash and be more expensive and, more importantly, take much longer than acquiring an existing truck manufacturing and distribution operation.

In Conclusion

As we have seen in this second chapter, where there is great volatility in terms of sales and resulting cash flows a key vital issue from the ERF case study is the careful management of both the working capital cycle and capital expenditures. The maintenance of prudent debt/equity ratios to mitigate potential business risk during economic downturns is another vital factor in any business..

3

CASH FLOW AND THE BANK

See the Capital Cycle Diagram opposite.

    In the first chapter, we focused on some macro and strategic issues affecting cash flows. Now we shall concentrate on the lower half of the capital cycle diagram. The working capital cycle of a manufacturer is illustrated. The traditional definition of working capital is of course well known as current assets minus current liabilities. Within this the bank overdraft would feature as a current liability. However if we think about this very carefully ***the bank is not actually a working capital item in any business*** - but is in fact a working capital provider if the business is cash negative within the cycle, or a working capital recipient if the business generates positive cash flow from the working capital cycle. The estimating and monitoring of cash flow requirements is therefore a key issue for any type of business be it large or small, as we have previously seen. Where a business requires funding by way of debt for working capital or capital expenditure purposes, the bankers concerned will be scrutinizing cash flows as a prime area within their credit-risk appraisal. It follows that the first key to the control of working capital is to *minimize the amount invested* in the working capital cycle to reduce the potential need for external financing.

Managing the Cash Flows

Within the cycle, creditors are unusual in that during the period of credit taken they represent an interest-free loan to the company, the benefit of which arises directly as a consequence of trading. Thus it is in the interests of most businesses to maximize the free-credit period available from creditors. This does not

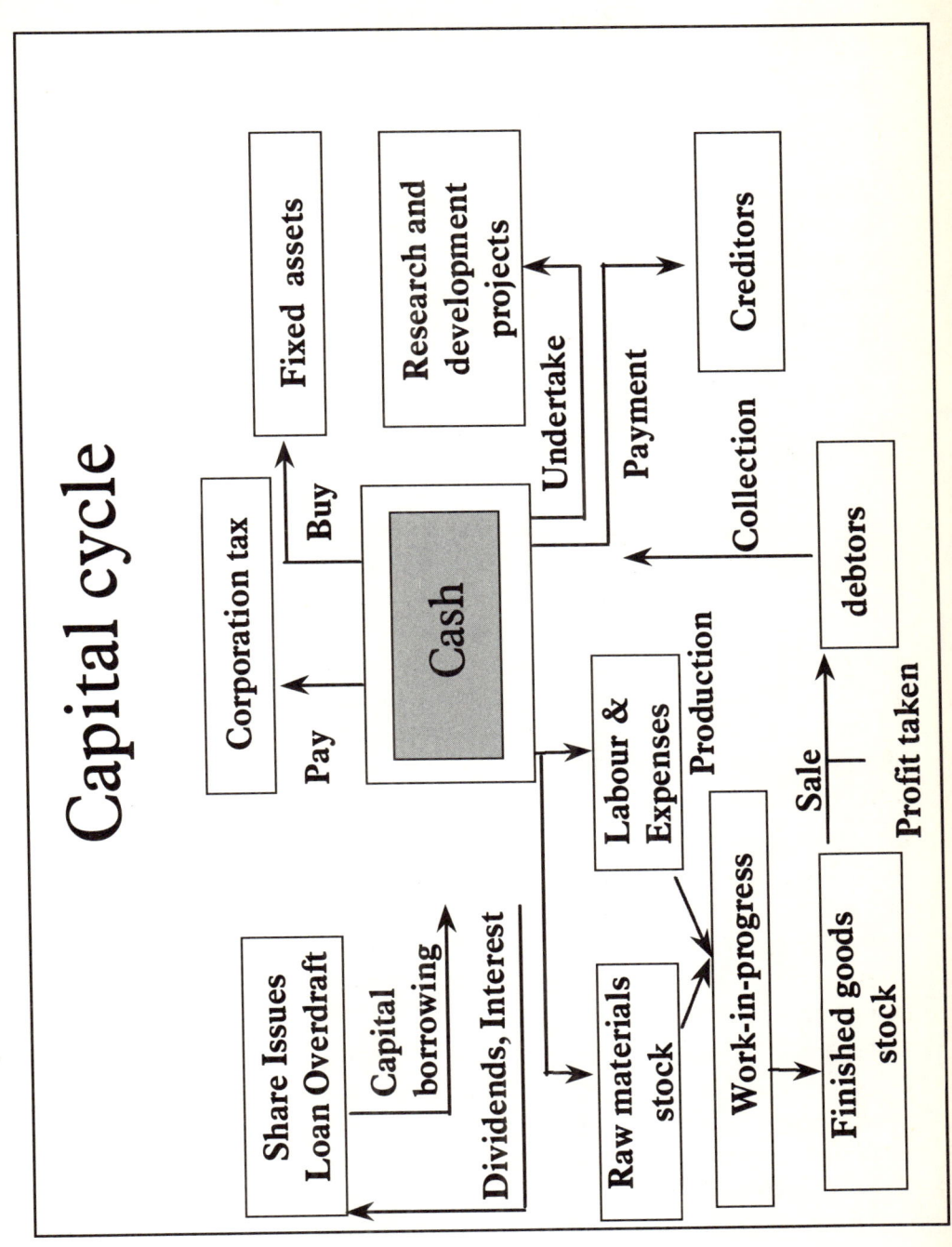

necessarily mean extending the period before payment beyond the agreed terms with creditors as this will have an impact on the business in three ways. It will affect its credit rating adversely, it could result in suppliers increasing prices to compensate for the funding cost of the delayed payment, and finally creditors may withdraw from supplying while taking action to petition the business for non-payment.

Where creditworthiness is not an issue, it can be possible to negotiate extended terms with key suppliers, particularly if the business is large. This can be particularly beneficial if more traditional forms of finance such as bank loans are difficult to obtain.

Labour costs are usually the second biggest input into the manufacturing process after raw materials, consequently the cash flow involved can be substantial. There are a variety of strategies available to the business experiencing problems, ranging from a temporary cut in wages imposed across the board to substantial redundancies across all functions within the business. Also, there is usually some scope to temporarily defer the paying over of deductions to the government, although this is increasingly the subject of ever more onerous legislation with the penalties involved and giving the recipient government department the right to charge interest. Accordingly such actions should be contemplated only after taking appropriate advice regarding the risks involved.

Overheads are the remaining component of expenditure in all businesses. There is usually scope to cut overheads in most businesses which are experiencing a shortfall of cash for the first time. The larger the business, usually the more redundant expenditure will be discovered. Overheads can be split into various types:

- Establishment expenses represent the costs of occupation of property. A variety of strategies are available, ranging from the reduction in the space occupied within a building so offering the option of renting off or selling the surplus space, to the elimination for as long as is necessary of all non-essential costs such as office cleaning, decoration and non-essential maintenance.

- Production costs require constant review if a business is to remain absolutely competitive at all times. Where this process has been neglected technology may provide numerous opportunities to substitute newer faster machinery to replace older more cumbersome machinery employing more people to operate. Using HP finance it may be possible to reduce costs substantially without *any* direct cash outflow. This method is particularly effective where the demand for the product being manufactured is fairly consistent.

Measuring the output of labour is particularly important; if this is not done you can find that the time required to complete work seems to expand to match the paid hours available. The introduction of labour productivity measurement alone can result in significant increases in productivity, as can the monitoring of all reasons for any non-productive time arising each working week.

An analysis of maintenance costs can reveal useful information and expose specific machines and operations which may be absorbing disproportionate amounts of maintenance time and effort. Simply ceasing the use of such machines may be the answer. Alternatively minor modifications or reorganization may also be sufficient to save much wasted resource and time.

A thorough review of all the components of production costs may expose areas where an item or service might be more cheaply sourced outside the business.

- Selling expenses need to be monitored as it is important to ensure that the costs of marketing and selling the businesses output are well matched to the areas of margin generation which are strategic to the business. Possibly the traditional markets served by the business have been superseded by newer markets without any refocusing of the businesses sales resources.

- In times of cash constraint, administrative expenses and thus the administrative areas of the company come under increasing pressure to perform better with less and less resource. Capital expenditure and discretionary expenses are cut and there is an increased need for cash flow management, information and control. Paradoxically this could mean it may be necessary to add resource to the administration function rather than remove it. Liquidity problems usually arise due to lack of management foresight; consequently, in such companies, there are often no budgets or forecasts. These therefore require preparation as the problems develop, in addition to the cash flow information mentioned earlier, so further stretching what is likely by this point to be an insufficient resource within the administration function.

- Stock represents significant value invested in the real or non-cash items within a business. Again there are certain areas to consider when reviewing any situation where working capital needs appear to be becoming excessive.

Raw materials represent the basic material inputs to any manufacturing process. The first thing to consider initially is: Is purchasing under control? Who can purchase and what can they purchase? Where purchasing is not in control cash can easily be squandered in buying the wrong thing, buying too much of a thing, buying at the wrong time (usually too early but sometimes too late!) and buying at the wrong price. It is important to remember that a liability is incurred when a contract is entered into (i.e. when the order is given to the supplier), *not* when the cheque is signed.

Also it is important that the work in progress and finished goods are reviewed regularly.

The key control here is regular stocktaking. This tells us two things: firstly, that the stock we thought we had is still actually there, and secondly it tells us how long we have in stock and in work in progress. Older stock is the less likely to be sold for cash at anything near its real value. Provisions are commonly made in accounts for slow moving, obsolete and damaged stocks. In cash flow terms, all of them represent mistakes or lack of foresight on the part of management. Again many businesses neglect to review stocks and take appropriate action on their findings.

- Fixed assets are the other major area of non-cash investment. The usual response to problems with cash flows is to put an embargo on all capital expenditure. If the company or group involved is relatively well invested this may not cause too many problems. However, it can be counterproductive in companies where new investment may be the only way of improving performance in the short term. In larger manufacturing businesses it is common to find substantial amounts of non-essential machinery that have been retained hoping it might come in useful in the future, or because it may yield spares for other machinery. Selling off non-essential machinery can often yield a useful cash contribution.

  The premises themselves occupied by the business can also provide a useful cash injection, if necessary by downsizing or relocation of the existing business or sale and leaseback arrangements. If surplus space can be split off it may be possible to rent it out. Finally there may be development value in old premises, particularly if situated strategically to large centres of population.

- Debtors are the last element of the working capital cycle prior to the realization of goods back into cash. Here the first thing to consider is speed of collection. Is it reasonable? Can it be improved? In the UK a reasonable collection is anything from 45-75 days, depending on the typical sector payment terms and quality of the customer covenant. Numerous methods can be used to chase debt including dedicated credit controllers, extensive use of the telephone, and suing in the last resort. More subtle is to consider carefully if the terms of business can be modified to provide more customer incentive to pay more promptly, or whether improvements can be obtained by more effective forms of distribution to the end user of the product. It may be possible to control distribution more carefully so that customers generate more margin from the product sold, hence improving their cash flow and ability to pay. Finally it may be possible to sell a product for cash rather than on credit by changes in the product offering.

The Pattern of Cash Flows

The second key component of managing cash flows is to understand the pattern of the working capital behaviour of the business in which we are interested. This will enable us to anticipate the likely problems in control and management which might arise.

While each of these factors is determined largely by the company's industry characteristics, each is also controllable to some extent by management. For example, most companies can, through their marketing policies, take actions to stabilize both unit sales and sales prices. However, this stabilization may require either large expenditure on advertising or price concessions to induce customers to commit to purchasing fixed quantities at fixed prices in the future. Similarly, firms can reduce the volatility of future input costs by negotiating long-term labour and materials supply contracts, but they may have to agree to pay prices above the current price level to obtain these contracts.

The essential relationships between suppliers, buyers and competitors will therefore shape a company's terms of trade – i.e., how quickly it pays suppliers, collects cash from customers and turns its raw materials into finished goods. This can be examined in more detail featuring the 1980s recessionary period in the UK by looking at the following comparisons of working investment or, as it is often termed, net working assets.

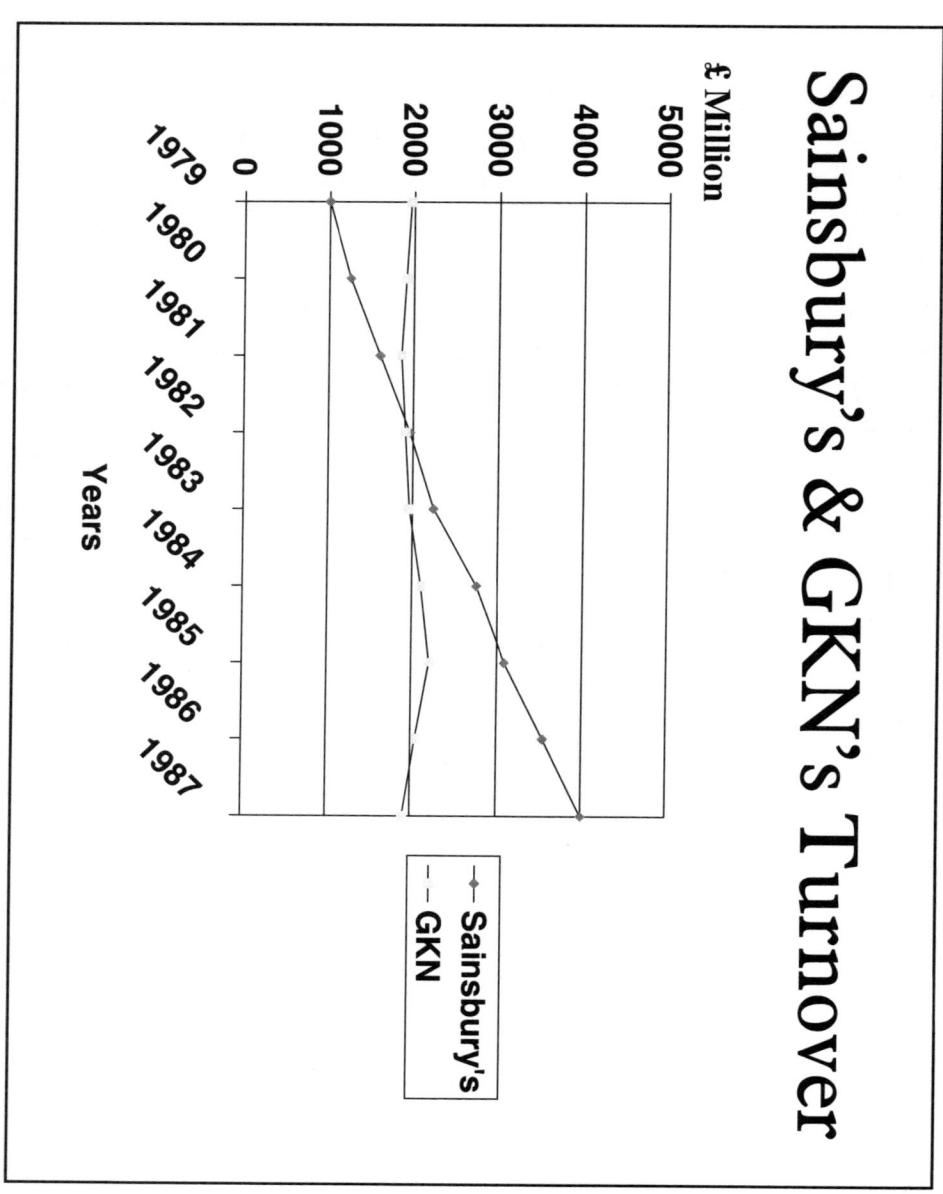

GKN v. Sainsbury

The finance requirement in the cash conversion cycle is known as the NET WORKING ASSETS or working investment. The amount of net working assets is therefore calculated as follows:

NWA = (Trade Debtors + Stock) - (Trade creditors)

The period I am specifically contrasting for Sainsbury and GKN is between 1979 and 1983, encompassing the last recession.

Sainsbury's turnover can be seen to be steadily advancing, whereas that of GKN is flat, and in fact, if you deducted inflation, the turnover was actually in decline.

Calculating Sainsbury's NWA requirement in 1983 actually shows a negative NWA requirement and they are in fact cash generators within the working capital cycle to the extent of £3.40 for every £100 of sales taking place within the stores – no wonder they have been able to embark on new superstore developments! See Table opposite.

On the other side (GKN as you would expect from a manufacturer) have a NWA requirement in 1979 of 28% for every £100 of sales – they are a cash consumer in terms of the NWA cycle. However, by taking very positive action and focusing on their cash management, they were able by 1983 to reduce this burden to 18%. This is a very significant saving when you consider their large turnover figure and the cash values committed to stock.

See Table overleaf.

Sainsbury's Working Capital

1983	#m
Sales	2293
+ Stock	142
+ Debtors	17
+ Cash $\left(\dfrac{2293 \times 2}{365}\right)$	13
- Creditors	(251)
W/C	(79)
$\dfrac{(79)}{2293} \times 100 =$	(3.4%)

GKN
Working Capital

#m	1979
Sales	1961
Stock + Net Debtors/Creditors	518
	28
Working Capital Requirement	546

$$\frac{546}{1961} \times 100 = 28\%$$

A Quote from GKN 1983 Report and Accounts: "Working capital has remained under close control and improved for the fifth sucessive year – in spite of capital expenditure of some £28 million higher, there was a net cash inflow in the year of £8.5 million."

Net Working Asset Financing

The net working assets need to be financed either by short-term bank overdraft, medium-term loan or from the shareholders by way of equity.

(a) Permanent NWA – the minimum amount required to support a base level of stock to ensure production runs smoothly.

(b) Increase in NWA resulting from sales growth – NWA goes up in proportion to increased sales (unless the operating cycle is shortened by increased efficiency and lower inventory or by collecting debtors earlier).

(c) Seasonal NWA requirement – this can arise monthly or yearly, perhaps because sales are seasonal (e.g. toys, swimsuits) or if materials are seasonal (e.g. vegetables for canning).

Performance Comparison

Industry	Debtors	Stock	Creditors	NWA (Days)
Dept. Stores	29	54	40	4
Textiles	80	85	72	93
Leisure	88	54	109	33
Food Retailing	26	25	46	5
Contractors & Construction	56	160	18	138
Mechanical Engineering	95	64	81	78
Aerospace	88	80	84	84
Household Appliances	77	58	69	66
Publishing & Print	102	55	81	76

NWA Survey Data – 450 Companies

This survey gives an indication **only** of the likely contrasting levels of NWA, this time in terms of the days within the cycle, between differing sectors. The survey was a random sample in terms of size of company and geographical location. It is important to note that the sample was specifically UK based. As you would expect, food retailing comes out the lowest at 5 days NWA, and Contractors and Construction the highest at 138 days, due to the length of the stock periods.

A thorough understanding of cash conversion cycles is essential because any cash left from the operating cycle will be available for a company's investment and financing activities. An understanding of business risk and the business cycle will help the corporate manager to evaluate the long term investment decisions which a company makes, for example a new factory, production unit or the acquisition of another company. The forecast operating cash flow following the investment must be sufficient to service any financing associated with this investment, be it long-term debt, on which interest must be paid, or equity, on which investors' expectations must be met in terms of dividend payment and capital growth.

It is, therefore, important to analyse and evaluate the normal behaviours of cash flow in your particular business.

The next case from the United States illustrates and reinforces our earlier comments. The business was achieving growth but how could this be best managed in terms of cash flow?

CASE STUDY - DELL COMPUTER CORPORATION

Russ Banham reported in the December 1997 CFO magazine for senior executives that Dell's cash flow was the subject of close involvement by the Corporate Treasurer and the CFO.

Readers will see some dramatic results:

" In the here-today, gone-tomorrow business of computers, speed saves. Nobody knows that better than Tom Meredith of Dell Computer Corp. Since taking the CFO position at the Round Rock, Texas based company in 1993 - a job the former treasurer of Sun Micosystems Inc. nearly rejected because of the monumental challenge - Meredith has made velocity his mantra, and liquidity improvement his personal crusade. "I've always been grounded in the belief, right or wrong, that a company's focus on cash flow has nothing but a good impact on its operating performance," he says.

Dell's finance re-engineering effort was born of necessity in late 1995. The company's inventories were ballooning, accounts receivables were rising faster than its revenue growth rates, and asset management was undermined by several quarters of lackluster performance. Meredith notes "We needed to take the weight off the growth pedal and shift our focus to liquidity and profitability."

Turning Sales into Cash

"We sent out a consistent message to everyone to focus on three things - asset management, return on invested capital, and cash conversion". Speed is of the essence. "Basically, we focused on ways to convert what we sell directly to the marketplace as quickly as possible into cash", says Danny Caswell, manager of Dell's asset management department. To do that, Dell went its own way, involving everyone from employees to suppliers, from vendors to customers.

$$DSO + DSI - DPO = CCC$$

To determine improvements in return on invested capital, Dell's asset management team developed a set of internal benchmarks. Metrics included days sales outstanding (DSO), days in inventory (DSI), days payables outstanding (DPO). Add DSO and DSI, then subtract DPO, and you get the chief metric Dell uses to measure its liquidity: cash conversion cycle (CCC).

The metrics tell a compelling tale. Dell's cash conversion cycle has gone from an acceptable 40 days to a phenomenal minus 5 days in the fourth quarter of 1997. "Our biggest improvement was in the inventory area, which we drove down from 30-plus days to 13 days", Caswell says. "We analysed key inventory drivers to identify who was holding inventory and where. It turned out to be us almost exclusively.

Shorter Receivables, Longer Payables

Improved inventory cycles were just part of the CCC turnaround. DSO was pared from an already-respectable 42 days to 37 days over the one-year period. What did the trick? It was new collections tools provided to Dell's customer financial services department to improve order processing and collection activities. Dell also was able to make similar headway in the DPO metric, which increased from 33 days to 54 days. "We were often paying our bills before the negotiated terms", Caswell recalls.

SNAPSHOT

TREASURY OPERATIONS
Company: Dell Computer Corp., Round Rock, Texas
Business: Computer Manufacturer
Revenues (1996): $7.7 billion
Number of Employees: 14,000

BEST PRACTICES
1. Balanced priorities of liquidity, profitability, and growth by emphasizing return on invested capital and reduced cash conversion metrics.
2. Invited employees, suppliers, vendors and customers into its educational campaign to develop cash conversion strategies.
3. Designated its asset management team responsible for reengineering the financial services training curriculum to improve functions and reduce errors in order processing and collections.
4. Centralized the treasury function for domestic and foreign operations.
5. Made business units fully responsible for credit and collections processes.
6. Developed systems to improve vendor processing, customer processing, and accounting processing in tandem with the reengineering of treasury operations.

KEY METRICS	Q4 1996	Q4 1997
1. Days sales outstanding	42	37
2. Days sales in inventory	31	13
3. Days payables outstanding	33	54
4. Cash conversion cycle (days)	40	-5

Source: Dell Computer Corp

Cash Flow and the Bank

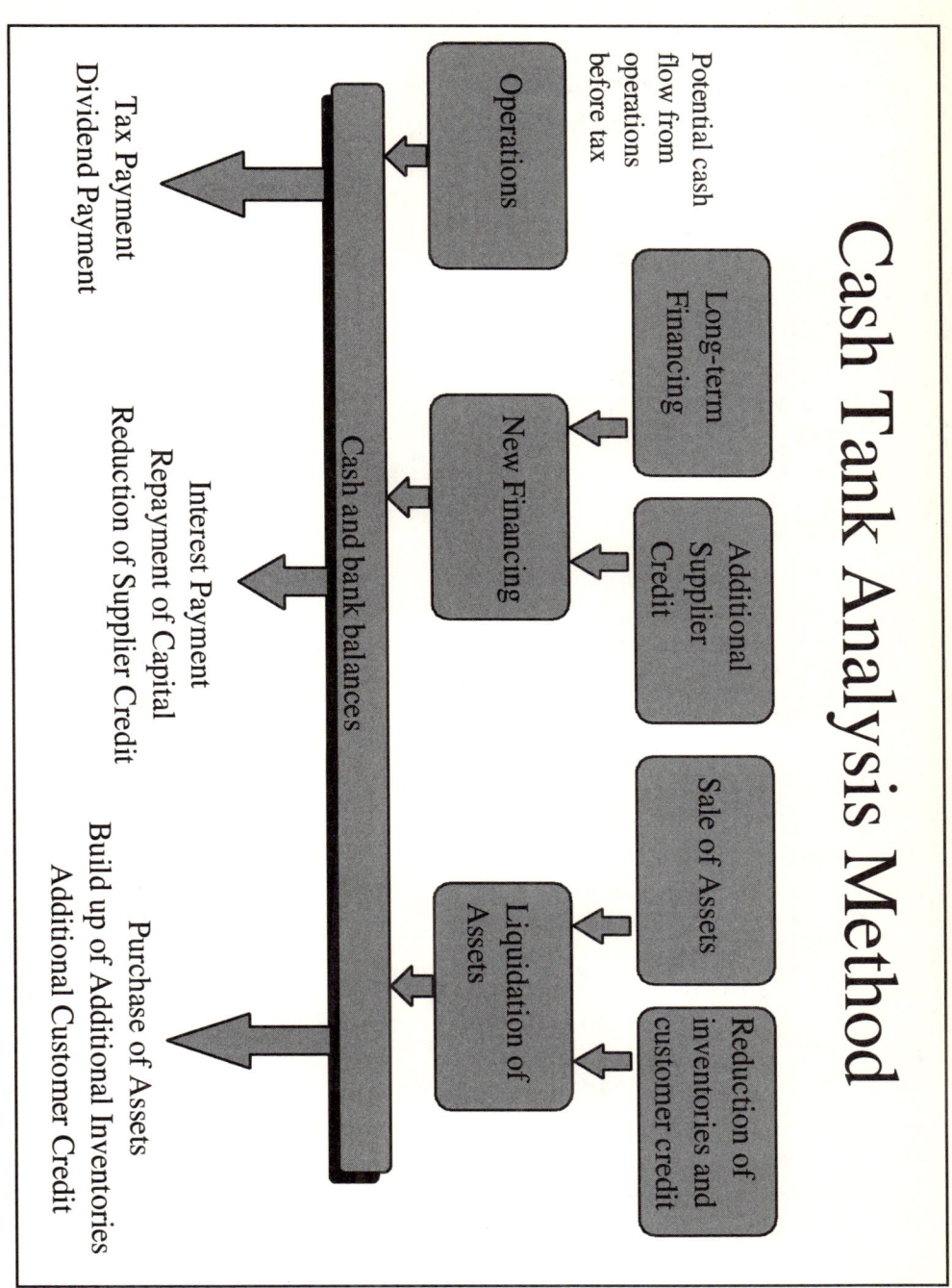

Assessing the Vulnerability of Cash Flows

The third key issue is to examine the overall cash flow appearance of a business and see whether the cash flows are quickly vulnerable to deterioration. See Cash Tank diagram on previous page.

	A £'000	B £'000	C £'000
CASH GENERATION			
Cash from operations	2,000	1,000	500
Working capital investment	(500)	(700)	(700)
Fixed asset investment	(300)	(300)	(300)
Funding costs	(450)	(500)	(550)
Taxation and dividends	(250)		
Cash generated/absorbed	500	(500)	(1050)
FUNDING MOVEMENT			
Short debt increase/decrease	(350)	350	800
Long debt increase/decrease	(150)	150	250
Equity increase/decrease			
Other non-trading flows			
Net funding movement	(500)	500	1,050

As you can see company A is a positive cash generator. From the £2m cash generated from operations there is sufficient to invest £500,000 into the working capital cycle, £300,000 into fixed assets, £450,000 in interest to debt providers, pay £250,000 in tax and dividends and still have a surplus of £500,000 to reduce debt.

Company B is achieving a poorer result. It is having to invest £1.5m more in working capital, fixed assets and debt servicing. It is generating £1m from trading. If this is a recent and temporary reduction in earnings the company should not suffer too much. If, however, this is a pattern which has remained present for two or three years problems are likely to occur. No company can trade like this indefinitely. It eventually runs out of cash reserves or debt providers.

Company C has problems and is not generating sufficient funds to cover its debt servicing costs. This is before even considering the sums expended into working capital and fixed assets in the current year. Debt is increasing to fund the underperformance.

Assessing the Volatility of Cash Flow

As we have seen before, the entry point of the cash flow is a derivative of the operating activities of the business. A useful tool in assessing the volatility of cash flows is to examine the relationship between sales, costs that tend to vary with output and the costs which are of a more fixed nature. The usual technique for this approach is to undertake a cost classification exercise and then construct a breakeven profile, which can then be reviewed in terms of volatility.

See overleaf for Break-even Analysis Chart.

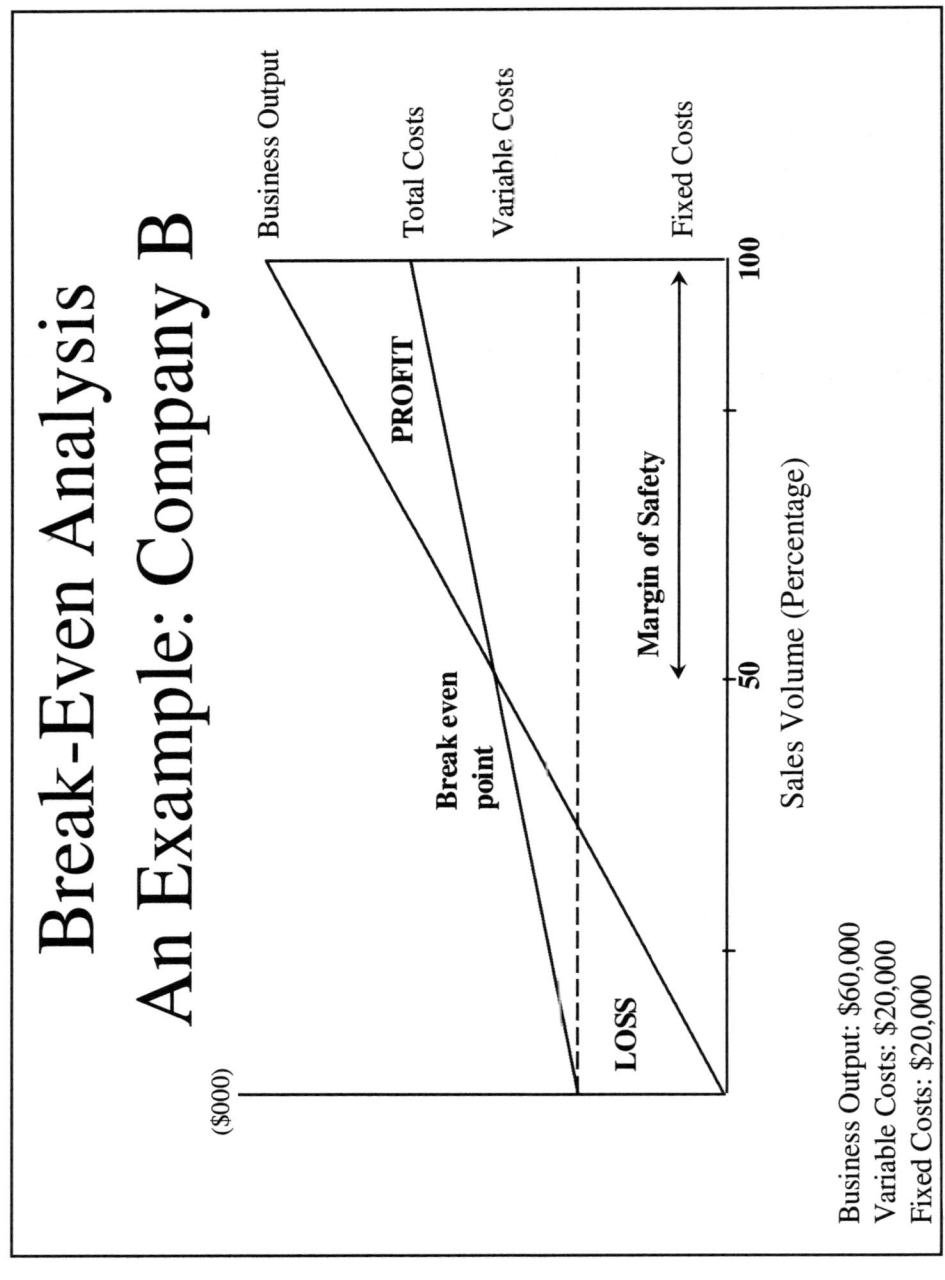

Comparing Cash Flows

A very useful exercise for any corporate manager is to compare cash flows with another corporate operating in the same sector. For the purpose of illustration, I have chosen two publicly quoted companies of senior ranking, both of whom manufacture soft drinks and have head offices domiciled within the UK.

BARR/NICOLS

I have illustrated, as an example, the 1996 figures, because the 1997 performance of AG Barr incorporates a 15 months trading period.

Both companies are showing tight working capital management, with net cash from operations positive at £9.9 m (Vimto) and £7.9 m (Barr): Vimto net cash flow position at £1.4 m after finance, taxation, dividends and capex; Barr cash negative at £5 m due to high capex at £9.1 m relating to new factory production facilities.

A.G. Barr Plc - Cash flow statement

	1996 £000	1996 £000
Net cash inflow from operating activities		7,962
Returns on investments and servicing of finance		
Interest received	-	
Interest paid	(733)	
Interest element of hire purchase paid	(309)	
Net cash outflow from returns on investments and servicing of finance		(1042)
Taxation		
Corporation tax paid		(1701)
Capital expenditure and financial investment		
Purchase of tangible fixed assets	(9121)	
Grants received	218	
Sale of tangible fixed assets	336	
		(8567)
		(3348)
Acquisitions and disposals		
Investment in associated undertaking		(100)
Dividends paid		(1591)
Net cash flow before financing		(5039)

Net Cash Inflow from Operating Activities

	1996 £000
Operating Profit	6083
Depreciation	4499
(Gain) on sale of tangible fixed assets	(22)
Government grants written back	(431)
Decrease/(increase) in stocks	(12)
(Increase)/decrease in debtors	1447
(Increase)/decrease in investment	4
Increase/(decrease) in creditors	(3,613)
Pension provision release	7
	7,962

JN Nicols (Vimto) Plc - Consolidated cash flow statement - Year ended 31/12/96

	1996 £000	£000
Cash inflow from operating activities		9933
Returns on investments and servicing of finance		
Investment income	284	
Interest element of hire purchase contracts	(8)	
Net cash inflow from returns on investments and servicing of finance		276
Taxation		(2856)
Capital expenditure and financial investment		
Purchase of tangible fixed assets	(3651)	
Investment in own shares	-	
Proceeds of Sales of tangible fixed assets	242	
Net cash outflow for capital expenditure and financial investment		(3409)
Acquisitions and disposals		
Purchase of subsidiary undertaking	1	
Proceeds on part sale of subsidiary undertaking	75	
Net cash inflow from acquisitions and disposals		76
Equity dividends paid		(2653)
Net cash flow before financing		1367

Reconciliation of Operating Profit to Net Cash Inflow from Operating Activities	
	1996
	£000
Operating Profit	9457
Depreciation	2393
Profit on sale of subsidiary undertaking	(15)
Profit on sale of tangible fixed assets	(46)
Write down of own shares	40
Increase in stocks	(532)
Increase in debtors	(1623)
Increase in creditors	259
	9933

The Effect of High Gearing on Cash Flow

How does high gearing influence cash flows? Cash flow payments of interest to debt providers represents cash leaving the cash-flow cycle of the business. If these values are high relative to a company's ability to generate cash, there is a constant danger that the lender's interest and fees will exceed the companies' ability to service them. Consequently there is tremendous pressure on the highly geared businesses to maintain a consistently high level of performance, because any reduction in cash generated can cause a decline into possible default of the company's debt arrangements and loan covenants.

It follows then that the gearing decision should be taken by management with a full understanding of the likely volatility of future cash flows. The most recent recession has shown us many corporate failures.

UK Company Receiverships

Year	No. of Receiverships (Last Recession)
1989	1187
1990	2634
1991	4112
1992	4333
1993	2845
1994	2040

If a business is very sensitive to changes in general economic conditions, this should be taken into account when considering the level of gearing appropriate to the business. In contrast, highly leveraged transactions based on food and consumer product businesses tend to be more successful because volumes tend to be only minimally affected when economic conditions change.

Cash flow and Capital Investment

So far we have examined cash flow generated from operations and then the absorption or generation of cash within the working investment. Next we shall look at the important area of capital expenditure, and in particular how we can evaluate the proposed investment.

Capital Expenditure: Introduction to Methods of Appraisal

There are four main methods of appraisal. They have in common a concern with cash flows. They all therefore require an evaluation of the initial cost, the running expenses, the estimated life of the project, and the income over the life of the project. Only cash items are included in the calculation of these factors. This means that depreciation is ignored, but the expected residual value of the item in the market place is included. Taxation, which may be a cash inflow or outflow, can have a significant effect on an investment decision and should always be included.

The four methods are payback, average rate of return, net present value, and yield or internal rate of return.

a. **Payback**

This method calculates the time for cash inflows to recoup the initial investment on the project. The payback period indicates to management the time that the investment is at risk: the shorter the length of the period to payback the better.

This method is widely used because it is simple to understand. It provides a clear indication of the time required to convert a "risky" investment into a safe one. It does not, however, pay any heed to several factors: the timing of cash flows, the situation after the payback period, and the return on capital invested.

b. **Average rate of return**

This method calculates the average annual net cash inflow as a percentage of the initial cash outflow. This may be represented by the formula:

Cash Flow and the Bank

$$\frac{\text{Average annual net cash inflow}}{\text{Initial cash outlay}}$$

This provides an entirely different kind of yardstick, which indicates the return earned on the capital employed. This method also has the advantage of simplicity, but continues to ignore the timing of cash flows.

c. Net present value

Money said to have a time value of £1 today is worth more than £1 in a year's time because it can be invested to earn interest. How much more it is worth will depend upon the rate of interest it can earn during the year. If it can be used to buy stocks or bonds paying 10 per cent per annum, then it will be worth £1.10 in one year's time. Expressed another way, £1 received in one year's time is equivalent to 91p today (91p + 10% = £1).

To arrive at a proper appraisal an allowance must be made for the timing of cash flows, and this is done by reducing the value of future incomings and outgoings to their present-day worth, using an appropriate rate of interest. This process is known as "discounting" and the factors may be calculated using the formula:

$$\frac{1}{(1+i)^n}$$

where i is the rate of interest and n the number of years. In practice, it is much easier to look up the figures in discounting tables.

To provide an additional assessment of the merits of each investment, the discounted inflows can be related to the original outlay to complete what is known as the "profitability index". The project with the highest profitability index is to be preferred.

d. Yield or internal rate of return

This is a refinement of the last method. It is used when managers wish to know the discount rate that exactly equates cash inflows with the outlay. This is sometimes to be preferred to assuming a rate. The calculation is more time-consuming because it involves using a trial and error method on at least two rates until the two figures are equal.
This rate can then be compared with, say, the rate of any borrowed money which may be required to finance the project or the company's average cost of capital. See overleaf.

Cash Flow: Capital Expenditure Decisions - Payback Method

Cash Price and all other initial Costs	Machine A #50.0	Machine B #50.0	Machine C #70.0
Net Cash Inflows			
Year 1	5.0	15.0	10.0
Year 2	10.0	25.0	10.0
Year 3	15.0	15.0	20.0
Year 4	20.0	5.0	20.0
Year 5	20.0	5.0	30.0
Year 6	15.0	-	20.0
Year 7	-	-	10.0
Residual Value (at end of last operating year)	1.0	-	10.0
	86.0	65.0	122.0
Payback (Years)	4	2 2/3	4 1/3

(All figures in 000s)   Ref.M.A.Pitcher

Discounting Cash Flow Method

	10% Discount Value	Machine A Actual Value #	Machine A Present Value #	Machine B Actual Value #	Machine B Present Value #	Machine C Actual Value #	Machine C Present Value #
Initial Cash Outflow	1	50,000	50,000	50,000	50,000	70,000	70,000
Net Cash Inflows (Yr)							
1	.909	5,000	4,545	15,000	13,635	10,000	9,090
2	.826	10,000	8,260	25,000	20,650	10,000	8,260
3	.751	15,000	11,265	15,000	11,265	20,000	15,020
4	.685	20,000	13,660	5,000	3,415	20,000	13,660
5	.621	20,000	12,420	5,000	3,105	30,000	18,630
6	.564	15,000	8,460	–	–	20,000	11,280
7	.513	–	–	–	–	10,000	5,130
Residual Value		1,000	564	–	–	2,000	1,026
		86,000	59,174	65,000	52,070	122,000	82,096

SHORTCOMINGS OF APPRAISAL METHODS

Having completed an example, one shortcoming is immediately obvious: not all methods give the same answer. The final choice must be made in the light of all the circumstances; it is a matter for managerial judgement as to whether the security of a short payback outweighs the disadvantage of lower profitability.

The forecasting of cash flows can also pose serious problems. Because of the longer-term nature of most capital investment, it is often extremely difficult to project timings and amounts for cash inflows and outflows, particularly during the later stages of the project. This can easily render any appraisal meaningless. Delays in installation of even comparatively simple machinery can quickly cause large variances from the plan, and escalating costs can rapidly eat up margins. In many cases, some proportion of the net cash inflows is represented by expected cost savings, and these are often much more difficult to realize in practice than they are on paper. The machine that was intended to dispense with the services of ten operatives and increase productivity by 30 per cent often looks much less economical after the first year of operation.

It is vital to take all cash items into account when completing the appraisal. It is easy to forget the cost of any additional working capital the project may require, particularly in the area of work-in-progress. Occasionally, new equipment can provide a reduction in the need for working capital and this should not be overlooked as a cash inflow or lower cash outflow.

Monitoring and Liquidity
The monitoring of liquidity can be easily carried out by using a control form such as the example of ABC Ltd opposite, with the figures being compared to the last available audited accounts.
With such a form the listing of figures for debtors, stock, creditors, etc. from the latest available annual accounts forms a useful base for comparison with current figures on a month-to-month basis. The bank balances used should be as per the company's books. Sales per annum and sales per month have been included. This information will enable you to monitor current activities at a glance. Capital expenditures or disposals should be minuted – because they will of course have an effect on liquidity movements. The current assets total line A should then be compared with the agreed banker's lending cover formula to ensure compliance.

Monitoring Form

COMPANY NAME: ABC
AGREED FORMULA: 2.5 times debtors plus stock

From Company Books

	Annual Accounts 31/12/X5 #	Jan #	Feb #	Mar #	Apr #	May #	June #
Current Assets							
Cash	2,500	1,800	2,600	1,500	2,800	3,200	1,800
Debtors	484,500	472,653	486,152	517,250	586,220	570,185	526,590
Stock	120,000	135,500	140,200	120,700	115,800	112,100	110,500
Total (A)	607,000	609,953	628,952	639,450	704,820	685,486	638,890
Current Liabilities							
Bank	115,850	108,950	120,680	105,700	102,600	100,849	98,774
Creditors	192,180	210,525	200,520	225,600	210,723	202,576	197,821
Total (B)	308,030	319,475	321,200	331,300	313,523	303,425	296,595
Net of Totals (A-B)	296,970	290,478	307,752	308,150	391,297	362,060	346,795
Capital Expenditure (Disposals)	10,000						30,000
Sales Record	2.4 m per annum	215,280	325,650	350,320	325,000	328,520	255,650

CRITICAL ANALYSIS OF VARIATIONS

As well as monitoring the bank compliance, the monitoring form is also useful in highlighting the net current asset movement position (net of totals: A - B), as the example shows:

(a) The formula was 2½ times cover by debtors and stock - this was easily maintained each month.

(b) The net current assets position (A- B) shows an improving trend from January to May but suddenly drops back in June. (Why did this occur?)

Enquiry reveals £30,000 spent on a new machine.

However, comparing the June end position with the opening figures shows an improvement of (£376,795 - £298,970). Although this does not always represent a profit figure, it does show as a healthy sign - this positive movement can only be caused by profits earned or funds injected or sale of fixed assets or a combination of all three, unless there has been some significant changes in the terms of trade.

Equally, if the movement was negative (as occurred from May to June), further enquiry would be justified.

(c) The annual sales of £2.4 million average out at £200,000 per month. Monthly sales recorded on the form look good in comparison, and it will be interesting to see the full 12 month's picture. Sales also show a seasonality trend with peak sales in March.

ADDITIONAL ANALYSIS

You will have seen how important it is to any business to fully analyse the cash tied up in the figures presented on the liquidity monitoring form. For this reason it is suggested that the following additional analyses are made.

Debtors

This figure needs breaking down into normal trade, inter-company, and doubtful debts. Care should be taken not to include any debts which have been factored under a factoring agreement. Further, it is useful to get an indication of debtor spread and debtor control.

Debtor analysis

DEBTOR	TOTALS	AGE (days)				REMARKS
		Current	30	60	90	
£1000 and over						
Others						
Percentages	100%	%	%	%	%	

Debtor analysis by major customer account

NAME	Total balance	Current	30 days	60 days	90 days	REMARKS
Totals						

Stock

This figure is a difficult one for many businesses to provide. Frequently there will be many differing stock-lines and the only accurate way is to carry out a physical stock-check. However, this difficulty can be overcome if the stock-file is computerized. Often, though, in practice you will have to make an estimate based on stock movements during the month. A quarterly or even monthly physical stock-take should be encouraged to give a clear indicator of the actual stock position. A further complication occurs in businesses where there is on-going product manufacture or job contracts - then it will be necessary to estimate work-in-progress.

Also stock can be invoiced from a supplier subject to reservation of title (Romalpa terms). This reservation means that goods supplied remain the property of the supplier until he is paid. Again this should be noted.

Analysis of manufacturing stock

Month Ended		
Stock	£	as a %
Raw materials		
Work in progress		
Finished goods		
Total stock*		
*Reservation of title £........		

It is useful, when stock is physically checked and valued, to mark the stock figure on the debenture monitoring form accordingly.

Creditors

In addition to age analysis (below), it is also very useful to split the creditors total into normal trade and preferential. In business we always need to keep a watch on the prioritization of our creditors. We should establish if there are any set-off trading positions between creditors and debtors which might lead to counter-claims.

Creditor analysis

CREDITOR	TOTALS		AGE			REMARKS
		Current	30	60	90	
£1000 and over						
Others						
Percentages	100%	%	%	%	%	

Creditor analysis by major customer account

CREDITOR	TOTALS		AGE			REMARKS
		Current	30	60	90	
Trade:						
Preferential creditors						
VAT						
PAYE/NIC						
etc.						
TOTALS						

The management of these critical factors and their impact on the bank will be studied in the following case studies, which illustrate differing businesses in terms of size and business sector.

4
CASH FLOW AND THE BANK: ILLUSTRATIVE CASE STUDIES

CASE STUDY 1 - LENDAL HOLDINGS LTD

Now we will look at a business/banker cash flow relationship on a fairly small business which runs into cash flow problems for a variety of reasons, as you will see. This case study features both Pig breeding and the related industry of Pig-building manufacturing; both sector activities are undertaken by Lendal. Readers are urged to carefully study the cash-flow implications within the corporate specialist's report - see page 108.

Background - December 1997

The Accounts Clerk at Lendal peered gloomily over the latest statements from the Bank, following on from a terse telephone call from the Bank Manager of branch X. This was not the first call and there had been many cash flow difficulties of late. After summarizing the latest figures, the bank account trends were as follows:

BANK A/C TRENDS LENDAL HOLDINGS

		Worst	Best	Av Bal	Limit	Dr T/O
1997	JAN	92326D	47578D	66528D	171000D	67268D
	FEB	94368D	35200D	59119D	171000D	50253D
	MAR	82037D	37940D	59864D	171000D	55996D
	APR	106384D	77484D	92107D	171000D	43167D
	MAY	124576D	88249D	109173D	171000D	43612D
	JUN	147941D	126024D	138287D	171000D	35540D
	JUL	178824D	134831D	155332D	171000D	75544D
	AUG	196553D	173210D	185590D	171000D	33341D
	SEP	254647D	201254D	222618D	171000D	81607D
	OCT	230183D	186357D	211211D	171000D	66275D
	NOV	260692D	212026D	230033D	171000D	62789D
	DEC	264100D	216027D	241362D	171000D	61718D
		Dr T/O		*Av Bal*		
1995		384737D		38427D		
1996		694727D		56453D		
1997		680342D		129694D		

At the same time the bank manager was reporting to his regional controllers.

You will see from these figures that our bank position on this business looks very difficult and that I am far from happy with these trends and am bound to conclude that we have a cash-flow crisis on our hands!

As you know the Bank has paid the account up to £264,000 (Wednesday's overnight position) compared with the limit of £171,000, which actually formally expired last August!

The company have told me that they are having temporary cash flow problems but are sure that they are trading profitably. I have reservations as it is difficult to relate the profit claimed with the run of the bank account. Other areas which give cause for concern include:

- *I am worried about their financial controls exercised*
- *Their continuing hope of an up-turn in the pig industry*
- *Are all debtors good?*
- *Creditors - what level of pressure is being exerted? Are there any Writs outstanding?*

I have come to the conclusion that we must get a lot closer to their cash flow position in order to decide where we go from here. I know you share a lot of my concerns about where exactly do we stand and I wondered if the way forward would be to call for a visit from a Corporate Specialist who has extensive experience in cash-flow crisis situations?

In view of the mutual concern over cash flow, a Corporate Specialist was invited to visit the Company. Below are highlights of the report following the visit:

LENDAL HOLDINGS LIMITED
CORPORATE SPECIALIST REPORT

Group Balance as at 12.1.98	£286,120	Dr
Group Limit		£171,000

As requested, I am writing to report following my visit to the company.

The areas I looked at specifically were:

1. The Management Accounts produced as at 31 August 1997, and projections to 29 February 1998.
2. Quality of management and controls exercised.
3. The valuation of assets in a forced sale situation.
4. The products and associated industry.
5. Debtors.
6. Creditors. With the current high level of creditors, is pressure being exerted? Any Writs in existence?
7. The American and Canadian investments.

The Product Range
The basic set-up is manufacturing from Leeds Industrial Estate; a pig breeding, weaning and follow-on demonstration unit at Cliffe; a demonstration pig fattening unit at Cleckheaton; a newly established manufacturing business in Iowa, America, and a pig breeding and weaning demonstration unit at Calgary, Canada.

Lendal manufacture portable containerized pig units, which give an environmentally controlled producing and growing situation for pig farming. The price range varies from £5,050 to a maximum of £27,000 before VAT.

The advantage of the units to the farmer is the controlled environment, which produces a higher number of weaners per sow per annum to be sold, together

Cash Flow and the Bank: Illustrative Case Studies

with a better food conversion ratio.

The products look good, and demand has increased over the years:

| 1996 | Turnover | £524,263 |
| 1997 | Turnover | £1,095,273 |

Although the pig industry at the moment is pretty depressed, there is still a reasonable order book for units, together with repeat orders for the replacement of old pig housing units.

As regards Management, David Ball was away in America and I did not have the opportunity to meet him, and most of my discussions were with Ron Naylor whom I think would be best described as General Manager. He is technically competent, and certainly close to the technical production of the different pig units.

AUDITED CONSOLIDATED BALANCE SHEET AS AT 31 OCTOBER 1996

To illustrate the growth of the Companies, I have extracted the following figures from the consolidated Balance Sheet as at 31 October 1995 and 31 October 1996.

	1995	1996
Capital Employed:	£95,712	£148,415
and Consolidated P & L:		
Turnover:	£524,263	£1,095,273
Trading Profit For Year	(3.68%) £19,330	(5.2%) £57,327
(Before taxation)		

A more recent picture can be obtained from the following management documents:

MANAGEMENT CONSOLIDATED BALANCE SHEET AS AT 31 AUGUST 1997 AND PROJECTED BALANCE SHEET AS AT 29 FEBRUARY 1998

LENDAL HOLDINGS LTD AND SUBSIDIARY COMPANIES
PROJECTED BALANCE SHEET AT 29 FEBRUARY 1998
CONSOLIDATED BALANCE SHEET AS AT 31/8/97

	1997	1998	
Sources of capital employed			
Authorized	10,000	10,000	
Issued and fully paid			
1,000 ordinary shares of £1.00 each	1,000	1,000	
Reserves	113,824	138,004	
	114,824	139,004	
Minority interests in subsidiary companies	1194	1194	
Deferred taxation	56,000	56,000	
Directors' current accounts	14,750	14,750	
	186,768	210,948	
Application of capital employed			
fixed assets	435,691	447,068	
Less loans	35,160	23,156	
	400,531	423,912	
Current assets			
Stock	209,265	210,115	
Debtors	272,313	312,000	(includes USA
Cash in hand	9	8	99,900, Canada 14,200)
	481,587	522,123	
Less: current liabilities			
Creditors	451,825	405,087	
Bank overdraft	243,525	330.000	
	695,350	735,087	
Net current liabilities	(213,763)	(212,964)	
	£186,768	210,948	

This Management Balance Sheet as at 31 August 1997 has been prepared on the basis of a Statement of Affairs, and a stock take was carried out at the end of August. The figure of £113,824 for reserves was, therefore, a balancing figure. There are no supporting monthly Profit and Loss or Quarterly Profit and Loss Accounts to support this Balance Sheet.

The fixed asset valuation at £435,690 is analysed as follows:

SCHEDULE OF FIXED ASSETS - AS AT 31 AUGUST 1997

GROUP	Total	Land	Buildings	Plant & Machinery	Fixtures & Fittings	Motor Vehicles	Leased Fittings
Written down value	326,742	49,258	132,032	96,102	4,519	35,830	9,000
Sales for period	(12,880)	-	-	-	-	(3,880)	(9,000)
Additions	154,571	2,876	89,489	31,734	-	30,471	-
	468,434	52,134	221,522	127,837	4,519	62,421	-
Depreciation	32,744	-	-	19,175	564	13,004	-
	435,690	52,134	221,522	108,662	3,955	49,417	-

A total of £121,223 has been expended, mainly on buildings and plant and machinery at Cliffe, the main demonstration unit site, and Cleckheaton, the fattening unit site.

Stock as at 31 August 1997 totalled £209,265 as follows:

Stock & W.I.P. 31/8/97   £209,265

Analysis

L/Agricultural	76,451
Engineers	72,630
Pigs	56,027
Construction	4,157
	£209,265

This includes £63,000 attributable to work in progress, and the resulting balance of £145,000, some of which is subject to Romalpa terms (reservation of title). The Company could not identify the amount so affected.

The debtor figure at £272,313 includes the American and Canadian developments at £75,000. Also it is my understanding that a further deduction should be made of £27,000 as a provision for bad and doubtful debts. This reduces the debtor balance to £170,000.

The creditor figure at £451,825 includes the American and Canadian ventures, together with preferential creditors of around £30,000. It is not possible to identify the American and Canadian amounts.

Turning now to the projected Balance Sheet to 28 February 1998. This time the basis of compilation was to estimate profit and the resulting reserves balance, based on the turnover calculation and estimate of the net profit percentage. The problem here is that without a full analysis of overheads, bearing in mind the American and Canadian activities, it is impossible to conclude that the Company would have achieved a net profit percentage of around 5%, which would, on a £1.3M turnover projection, give the required level of profit to increase the reserves to the figure quoted at £138,004. The remaining figures have been progressed as can be seen - the debtor figure at £312,000 includes American and Canadian total investment projected of £114,100. The balancing figures on the Balance Sheet are creditors at £405,087 and Bank overdraft at £330,000. The increased Bank facility is therefore partly required to make a reduction in the creditor balance. The details of the Company's retained earnings calculation are given:

Retained Earnings

Sales   £

Agric. 21K per week x 26 weeks   546K

Engineering 4K per week x 26 weeks   104K

                                                       650K

                          @ 5% net profit 32.5K

Less

Loss on pigs (80 x £4 x 26 weeks)   8.3K

                                         NET   24.2K

MANAGEMENT INFORMATION AVAILABLE AS AT 31 DECEMBER 1997
(at time of my visit)

Debtors (Gross) £317,947

This will show a lower position of £193,000 after deducting £125,000 for the total American and Canadian investments as at 31 December. From this figure should be deducted £27,000 for provisions, giving the net debtor figure of around £166,000.

Creditors (Gross) £314,378

This does not include P.A.Y.E. (estimated 2 months - £30,000) or any accruals.

Ron Naylor told me that there had been two Writs levied against them, while he was away recently in America, but these had now been cleared up.

Sales turnover to 31 October is estimated at total sales across the group of £1,330,149. This level of activity is up on the previous year's turnover of just over £1M. As mentioned before, no monthly or quarterly Profit & Loss Accounts are compiled and, therefore, the only basis of profit projection would be to estimate at 5% net, giving a projected profit of £66,500 but this is, of course, only feasible if the level of overheads has been contained, and this must be questionable bearing in mind the American and Canadian ventures.

American Venture

This business was set up in America in 1997, and currently operates from a factory of 10,000 sq. ft. in Guttenberg in the State of Iowa. The factory employs 16 people, and they are currently manufacturing two pig units per week. According to Naylor there is a great demand for pig housing in America, particularly in Iowa due to the extremes in climatic conditions - the average number of weaners sold per sow per annum is only 14, whereas with the controlled housing environment, in excess of 20 weaners per sow per annum are being obtained at the demonstration unit at Cliffe. Capital was introduced by Lendal U.K. of $177,013, and capital provided by Double L (American Businessman) $105,000. At that time, a line of credit of $70,000 was negotiated with the Security State Bank of Iowa, supported by David Ball. I also understand that Ball purchased a house in Guttenberg for $85,000, on which there is a mortgage of approximately 50%. This house is also held as supporting security by the American Bank.

A Management Balance Sheet has been produced for the American investment as at 31 October 1997:

LENDAL HOLDINGS USA LTD
BALANCE SHEET – 31 OCTOBER 1997

Sources of Capital Employed

Capital provided by Lendal UK	$177,013.00	
Capital provided by Double L	<u>105,000.00</u>	282,013.00
Less setting up costs	<u>(130,987.00)</u>	<u>$151,026.00</u>

Application of Capital Employed

Fixed Assets

Leasehold building improvements	35,862.00	
Plant & equipment	21,811.00	
Office, fixtures, fittings & furnishings	<u>17,044.00</u>	$74,717.00

Current Assets

Credit on bank current account	6,236.00	
Stock (10 week purchases)	172,406.00	
Debtors (Accounts Receivable) (5 Week sales)	<u>85,276.00</u>	
	<u>$263,918.00</u>	

Current Liabilities

Creditors (7 week purchases)	117,609.00	
Bank loan	70,000.00	
Deficit on bank current account	-	
	<u>$187,609.00</u>	
Net Current Assets	76,309.00	
COMPANY NET WORTH		<u>$151,026.00</u>

There have been significant changes since that date in that Double L, the American, tended to be unreliable, and Lendal has bought out Double L by paying back the $105,000 for capital, plus $15,000 attributable to stock, giving a total pay out of 120,000 American dollars. This in turn led to an increased line of credit being obtained from the Security State Bank at $130,000, and Naylor told me that this is the maximum that the Security State Bank can lend to a corporate client. Capital employed, shown at $151,026 at a conversion rate of 1.42, gives a figure of £106,356.

The capital injection into America, plus the funds needed to buy out Double L, has meant that Naylor is preparing a Business Plan for when he intends to revisit America, mid- to end of February, to make a presentation to the Iowa Development Credit Corporation, and also the Norwest Bank to endeavour to raise additional monies to fund the manufacturing operation. He hopes to be able to return some capital back to the U.K. from this additional funding - I feel this is unlikely, as no Bank will be keen to lend additional funds on the basis that funds are to be returned to the U.K.

Canada

Two trial units are located in Calgary to show the potential of the Sow Units and Early Weaning Units. No formation statement is yet available for the Lendal Agricultural (Canadian) Limited position, but I understand that the formation will be as follows:

David Ball	25,000 Canadian dollars already invested by way of the Production Units.
Pierre Moreau	10,000 Canadian dollars
Alan Toles	10,000 Canadian dollars

On the basis of a 10,000 Canadian dollar investment each, David Ball should have 15,000 Canadian dollars to come back to the U.K. At a dollar conversion rate of 1.78, this equates to £8,426. At this stage there is therefore no intention to manufacture in Canada!

In Conclusion

It is my opinion that the Company's cash resources have been strained to the maximum, with the subsequent effect on the bank account balance and creditor position. To summarize, during 1997 they have further developed their Head Office; developed the fattening unit at Cleckheaton; developed the demonstration unit at Cliffe; entered a manufacturing situation in America, and a demonstration unit in Canada.

ASSET VALUATIONS

Estimates of valuations would be as follows:

Estimated Forced Sale Valuation

Factory Unit 40,000 sq ft approx at £1 per sq ft rental over 7 years £280,000	£140,000		
House 4½ acres of land, and pig accommodation for 176 sows to 11 weeks at £1,000 per sow place £176,000.	£50,000		
		£190,000	
Debtors as at 31/12/83	£318,000		
Less USA/Canadian and Provision	£125,000	£27,000	
NET		£166,000	£80,000
Stock		£209,000	
Less Work in Progress	£64,000		
(Less Romalpa)**	£145,000	£50,000	
			£320,000
Less Preferential Creditors estimated		£30,000	
		£290,000	Less realization costs

**(Reservation of title by suppliers)
Additionally, there is Ball's Unlimited Guarantee.
* **NB:** Fixed Assets P&M & Motor Vehicles discounted

Recommendations as to the way forward:

1. The Audited Accounts to 31 October 1997 to be produced as a matter of urgency.

2. Quarterly Profit and Loss figures, together with a stock take, should be carried out at 31 January 1998, to give an indication of progress for the first three months of the current trading year.

3. There has been no monitoring of liquidity figures, and this must be set up. I would suggest an urgent meeting with Ball, here at my office to discuss the future of his business connection vis-a-vis the cash flow requirements.

4. A short-term Cash Flow Forecast must be produced as a matter of urgency to pinpoint the way ahead, as regards cash requirements, bearing in mind the American and UK manufacturing set-ups.

5. If between the Auditors, Blower & Co, and the Company they are unable to come up with the information that is required, then I would recommend an independent firm of Accountants go in to help prepare the information which is desperately needed, before it is too late to come up with a rescue plan.

6. It is my opinion that the group of Companies are highly geared, cash flow is under extreme pressure and expansion must be **slowed down**, to give the Companies time to generate profits and positive cash flow which needs to be retained within the Business to give it a chance to survive.

Corporate Specialist 17 January 1998

Postscript for Readers:
Unfortunately it was all too late and before the business could get into more detailed analysis and cash flow projections with a survival plan, the business was petitioned by several creditors for non-payment. The bank would not advance more funds. The business went into liquidation.

CASE STUDY 2 - HR TRAILERS LTD

In any corporate, planning for future liquidity is essential. Cash flow forecasting will require little introduction to most business persons. It is easy for the equity investor to say "please prepare a cash forecast for the next 12 months". However the compilation of the document can be a long and arduous process. All businesses must of course preserve liquidity in order to meet cash commitments to the creditors, employees and the shareholders. A good forward order book will be useless if we do not have the cash needed to finance the production of our products. The ability therefore to be able to forecast cash movements and then monitor progress is a key requirement in business planning. A good place to start is by completing a cash flow worksheet:

> See Cash Flow Worksheet opposite

If the company sells mainly on credit, then the analysis of collections will be of crucial importance. However if you are selling mainly for cash, then more focus will be needed on disbursements. It is a question of fully analysing the cash profile of your business and committing it to the worksheet. From the worksheet, you can then evolve a monthly cash flow forecast and predict when cash will enter and leave your bank account. You will then know when it is best to purchase new equipment, take on more staff, etc.

We can now put this into practice by looking at an example case study, HR Trailers Ltd again featuring the cash flow relationship with the Bank. This case study concerns an established and successful business which runs into cash flow difficulties, presenting the business with problems in terms of future growth and the relationship banker with a series of cash flow decisions to make.

Part One – June 1989

In June 1989, HR Trailers Ltd. (HRT) asked the bank for an overdraft facility of £300,000 for general working capital purposes.

General Information

HRT sells trailers to the agricultural industry. Although these trailers look similar to any other, they are more suited to the transportation of agri-products and have a much greater capacity.

HRT has the exclusive rights to sell and distribute the specialist "Dimensions" trailer, which is manufactured by Sun Trailers (Far East) Inc. The "Dimensions" trailer is a minor product among Sun's trailer product range but the market niche it fits does require specialist knowledge and commitment to service. The main requirements of HRT's customers are for this type of powered trailer with a high capacity.

Cashflow Worksheet

	Year Ended				
	Profit before interest & Tax				
	Depreciation				
	Other Non-Cash Items				
A	**Gross Operating Cash Flow**				
	Movements in:				
	Stocks				
	Debtors				
	Trade Creditors				
	Pre-Payments				
	Accrued Expenses				
	Sundry C/L				
B	**Change in Working Investment**				
	Net Operating Cash Flow A +/- B				
	Interest Expenses				
	Dividends Paid				
	Long Term Debt (<12 months)				
	Net Cash Flow after Debt Service				
	Other Inflows and Outflows				
	Fixed Asset Expenditure/Disposals				
	Taxation				
C	**Net Cash Flow before Finance**				
	External Finance:				
	Increase in Equity				
	Short Term Debt				
	Long Term Debt				
D	**Net Movement in Cash***				

* Reconcile with Source Documents

HRT's machines are priced between £6,000 and £10,000 each, ignoring the cost of any customization requests. Terms are net 30 days for the basic machines to major establishments and commercial firms. Substantial deposits are taken on those orders for customized machines.

The delivery period for a customized machine is about 6 weeks, which includes the time taken to configure the trailer to the customer's requirements, while standard machines, if in stock, are dispatched within 48 hours after satisfactory credit enquiries. Customers are told, on placing their customized order and paying their deposit, that delivery will be in 6 to 8 weeks. If the delivery is later than this, customers can invoke certain conditions on the sale contract. They can start to claim discounts on their final invoice and, in some circumstances, cancel their order and receive their deposit back.

The company operates from a distribution unit, with offices above, in Sunderland. Storage capacity is fully utilized at these premises and will not support further expansion. The technical support and customization department is particularly cramped for space. There is an extensive range of new and second-hand specialist equipment in the factory, which is slowly being incorporated into a formal production line.

Management

The management team is young and consists of five people. The company was formed in 1986 by Nick Old and Lyn Black, who are joint managing directors and the major shareholders. The company's bankers have been B. Bank from its very beginning and there has never been a problem with the conduct of the account.

Nick Old and Lyn Black have been responsible for all aspects of the company's growth and for building up the present management team. They are supported by three senior people responsible for sales, technical support and distribution. Previously, they both held senior positions at Sun UK Ltd. Nick Old worked for Sun UK Ltd. for seven years rising to board level. He left because he saw no possibility of a meaningful equity participation. The company employs 19 people in total.

Nick Old identified in the very beginning the niche market for specialized machines and left Sun UK Ltd., which is a shareholder in HRT, with its blessing and an agreement to be its sole distributor in the UK to this specialized market. Despite the close association between the two companies and Sun UK's investment in HRT, Sun UK Ltd. has adopted a distinctly hands-off approach to the way in which HRT is operated. It is happy to see HRT push itself aggressively to the forefront of the market, making a name for itself and Sun's products.

Lyn Black is qualified in Business Studies and worked at Sun UK Ltd. for eight years as a marketing executive. Her role at Sun UK Ltd included advising on new products, market research and responsibility for a promotional budget of £2 million.

Nick is the communicator and driver of the business with ambition and energy to build the company. Lyn is equally ambitious but she acts as a foil to Nick, bringing a practical and steadying influence to the company.

Market

The company's customers range across a broad spectrum. The order book is currently healthy, with orders at capacity for the next four months. Throughout this niche market HRT has earned an excellent reputation by recommending and providing the right machine for each specific use. It offers a complete range of models and customizations based on the "Dimensions" trailer. With HRT's advantages of a skilled and knowledgeable sales force and full customization service, HRT is approaching the quality of service and product sophistication normally associated with main suppliers. .

Competitive Position

The company feels it has an added advantage over its competitors by providing quality service. The integration of distribution and customer service, from a local base within the UK, gives it added flexibility in fulfilling customers' orders. The company believes that its strong link with a major trailer manufacturer provides an effective barrier to new entrants to the market. The company aims to ensure that levels of stock of the basic machines are customer led.

Employment

Many of the workforce in the factory are school leavers trained from scratch by a core of HRT's skilled workers. The high turnover of workers in the factory has now reduced and stabilized. Labour relations appear to be good.

Expanding The Business - The Financial Issues

Early in 1989, HRT used its own resources to buy out the shareholders in Scottish Trailers, its principal competitor. Following this acquisition, HRT has become the market leader in the UK and the pressure on work space is increasing. The company expects sales to grow by over 100% across the board, as a result of the purchase of Scottish Trailers, and have approached Sun UK Ltd. concerning an equity investment in HRT.

After discussions Sun UK Ltd. earmarked a £1.4 million financial package to support continued expansion and growth of the company, on the understanding that HRT aims to seek a full Stock Market listing within the next 2 to 3 years. The Sun financial package is made up as follows:

	£
Share premium	308,400
Preference Shares	691,600
Total cash injected into HRT	1,000,000
(*Subordinated loan not yet drawn)	400,000
Total investment by Sun UK Ltd	1,400,000

* The subordinated loan has been made available for a maximum period of five years of trading. It is earmarked for specific purposes relating to the expansion of the business.

The Sun UK Ltd. investment is subject to various terms and conditions linked to a Stock Market flotation. The terms set out a timetable for the issue of shares and look for one-third of the shares to be issued within 12 months. In addition, sales are expected to achieve an annual growth rate of 7% above that resulting from the acquisition of Scottish Trailers. The shareholders, as at January 1989, are as follows:

	%
Nick Old	43.00
Lyn Black	43.00
Sun UK Ltd.	14.00
	100.00

Share options in the future may be made available to other senior members of the management team. The directors hope that the company will achieve a Stock Market floatation within the next 12 months. Extensive work has been carried out by a major firm of accountants and these accountants are now retained by Sun UK Ltd. to carry out "due diligence work".

Up until June 1989, the company has operated with strong cash flow and credit balances. However, even taking into account the new money invested by Sun UK Ltd., HRT has experienced a drain on its resources. This has partly been caused by buying out Scottish Trailers and partly by the increased working capital requirements resulting from the booming sales.

Financial Position

As at 31 March 1989, the company has retained profits of £686,000, net assets of £836,000 and credit balances with the Bank of £729,000. The Financial Report confirmed the first three months' cashflow forecast figures.

HRT's application for an overdraft facility in June 1989
HRT has approached the Bank for an overdraft facility of £300,000 to fund its increased working capital requirement resulting from continuing sales growth and the research and development expenditure. The company expresses its key trading advantages as:

- Its technical knowledge and back-up.
- The close relationship with its main supplier, Sun Trailers (Far East) Inc.
- The support and financial commitment of Sun UK Ltd. to the company through its minority share holding and investment.
- The company culture fostered by the management team.

The company appreciates that the general economic climate is on the edge of recession but believes for the following reasons that it has a very strong competitive edge. In order to reduce costs, many firms are prepared to invest in more advanced machines to cut down on manpower costs. The format of the business is well suited to the existing market conditions and is cushioned from the worst effects of the economic downturn because of its acknowledged position of service in this niche market. There is a potential to increase prices as a result of HRT's domination of this market. The integrated customization and selling operation provides low costs and flexibility.

The management team possesses a balance of skills and is highly motivated. The company has an enthusiastic and highly knowledgeable workforce.

Financial Information
The following financial information has been presented at the same time as the overdraft request. HRT's financial year ends 31 March.

Summarized Profit and Loss Account for 1987, 1988 and 1989

	12 months to 31.3.87 £000s	12 months to 31.3.88 £000s	12 months to 31.3.89 £000s	Forecast to: 31.3.90 £000s
Sales	259	1,945	4,659	9,164
Gross Profit	148	1,127	2,988	5,699
Profit before tax	69	202	810	1,165
Retained profit	65	140	686	1,149
Net Assets	68	458	836	2,299

Consolidated Balance Sheet as at 31 March 1989

This is the first Balance Sheet showing the inclusion of Scottish Trailers.

	£000s	£000s
FIXED ASSETS		806
CURRENT ASSETS		
Stocks	1,265	
Debtors and prepayments	834	
Bank	<u>729</u>	
	2,828	
CURRENT LIABILITIES		
Trade creditors	1,529	
Other creditors	634	
Corporation tax	281	
Hire purchase	51	
VAT	150	
	(2,645)	
NET CURRENT ASSETS		183
CREDITORS > 1 YEAR		
Hire Purchase	(153)	(153)
NET ASSETS		836
Share Capital		150
Retained Profits		686
		836

Forecast Profit and Loss Account for twelve months to 31 March 1990

	£000s
Sales	9,164
Material Costs	(3,465)
Gross Profit	5,699
Labour	(1,013)
Consultancy Fees	(673)
Advertising	(661)
Other Overheads	(2,187)
Profit Before Tax	1,165
Taxation	(408)
Dividend	(116)
Profit c/d	463

Forecast Balance Sheet as at 31 March 1990

	£000s	£000s
FIXED ASSETS		1,793
CURRENT ASSETS		
Stocks	1,745	
Debtors and prepayments	1,825	
Bank	23	
		3,593
CURRENT LIABILITIES		
Trade creditors	1,750	
Other creditors	435	
Corporation tax	395	
Hire purchase	50	
VAT	217	
		(2,847)
NET CURRENT ASSETS		746
CREDITORS > 1 YEAR		
Hire Purchase	(204)	(204)
Deferred Tax	(36)	(36)
NET ASSETS		2,299
Share Capital		1,150
Retained Profits		1,149
		2,299

Cash flow Forecast for the twelve months ending 31 March 1990

Month Ending	Receipts £000's	Payments £000's	Net Cash Flow b/f £000's	Bank Balance b/f £000's
April '89	802	1,024	(222)	507
May	1,150	1,244	(94)	242
June	1,644	1,634	10	148
July	1,825	1,905	(80)	158
August	1,121	1,270	(149)	78
September	949	737	212	(71)
October	881	1,173	(292)	141
November	1,128	986	142	(151)
December	1,194	1,052	142	(9)
January '90	1,194	1,242	(48)	133
February	1,004	1,066	(62)	85
March	746	766	(20)	23
	13,638	14,099	(461)	

The Bankers carried out their credit appraisal using a lending mnemonic (CAMPARI) as an aide to their review.

Outlined below, on the basis of the CAMPARI checklist, is the information available for an assessment of HRT's proposal for an Overdraft facility. The answers suggested here are not designed to be exhaustive but to cover the main issues which could be raised. You may well have additional points which you would want to raise yourself.

Assessment Using Campari

Character
Information gained – The management is young and consists of five people, some of whom have worked together before at Sun UK Ltd. They appear to form a good, enthusiastic and motivated team whose skills complement each other well. The company has always conducted its account satisfactorily. The workforce is young but has been trained by the company and appears now to be

operating well. The company appears to be aggressively sales led but may well be weak in terms of financial control.

Information required – There is very little information on the personal backgrounds of any of the management team. More information is required about their personal commitments, domestic circumstances and assets. There is some information about their business backgrounds but again this area could be explored further. From the information available, it is difficult to gain a feel for the business or the major people involved.

Ability

Information gained – The management team seem to be well qualified and experienced in their own spheres of operation. Although young, it appears to be a competent, as well as very ambitious, team. The company has captured a niche market not only by aggressive salesmanship but also by providing the right product at the right price. It has built up a solid reputation. Nick Old in particular seems to have had the ability to see the opportunity and to seize it. As a result of these factors, the growth of the company has been impressive. However, financial management and planning appears to be weak.

Information required – The management team has been able to cope well so far but how well will it react when problems occur? The ability of the management to cope with more difficult circumstances needs to be explored. There does not appear to be any very coherent plan for growth apart from acquisition. The following should be examined:

- What was the basis of the decision to purchase Scottish Trailers?
- What was the profitability of Scottish Trailers?
- Was Scottish Trailers borrowing and if so was this taken into account?
- To what extent was the viability of Scottish Trailers examined?
- What will be the impact on customer service to both existing HRT and new Scottish Trailers customers?
- How well organized is the business to cope with such growth?

Lack of cash flow planning seems to be indicated by the fact that the purchase of Scottish Trailers has driven the business towards an overdraft situation which is only now being addressed. Further to this, the business was already short of space before the takeover; the situation can only be worse now. How will this affect the performance of the company?

Margin

Information gained – The company has not been in the position of borrowing funds before so no interest margin has been set to date.

Information required – In considering what margin to apply and other fees, it will be important to examine the extent of any other borrowings. It will also be important to explore what the duration of the overdraft is expected to be, the pledging of collateral, the nature of the advance and its usage.

Purpose

Information gained - The overdraft is for working capital cash flow purposes in order to fund rapidly expanding sales and to fund research and development. This sales growth is mainly as a result of the purchase of Scottish Trailers. However, this has itself caused a considerable drain on cash resources and precipitated the requirement for an overdraft facility.

Information required – There is no very clearly defined purpose for the overdraft. To some extent it seems retrospective in terms of replacing funds drained out to purchase Scottish Trailers. If the overdraft is truly to be used to fund working capital requirements as a result of increased sales, evidence of market research to indicate the real potential for such growth over and above that which would be expected as a result of the takeover of Scottish Trailers should be examined. What is the state of the order book? What is the debtor position – are sales being converted into cash quickly enough?

Amount

Information gained – The request is for a £300,000 overdraft facility. The debt/equity ratio seems satisfactory in relation to the overdraft.

Information required – There is very little information about how the figure is assessed except that the cashflow forecast indicates a maximum cash shortfall of £151,000. If this is a realistic figure, there appears to be plenty of room for contingencies. It is important to find out and test the assumptions behind the amount requested and to conduct variance analysis to explore "what if" questions. There is no indication as to whether finance charges have been included. What other factors affecting costs have been taken into account? For example, with the absorption of Scottish Trailers and continued rapid growth, what is expected to happen to wage costs? What provision has been made for corporation tax? What plans have been made to alleviate the lack of space? *It is vital to find out about all these assumptions and to test them thoroughly.*

Repayment

Information gained – Repayment is ultimately to come from net cashflow surpluses as a result of sales growth.

Information required – If funds are to be provided, is an overdraft the most appropriate means of doing so? If repayment is to come from net cash flow surpluses, we need to question in detail the assumptions of the cash flow forecast. For example: How efficiently are funds collected? How have terms of trade changed following the purchase of Scottish Trailers?

Insurance
Information gained – The request for funds appears to have been made without the overt offer of any collateral. However, from the Balance Sheet, there is adequate cover for the Bank under Fixed and Current Assets.

The Outcome
In June 1989, the Bank agreed an overdraft facility of £300,000, to be charged at 1.75% over base rate, to assist with increased working capital requirements. This facility was secured by a mortgage debenture over the company's assets with 2-times debtor cover (under 90 days) as a lending covenant which ranks behind Sun UK Ltd.

As part of the agreement the following actions were to be taken:

- Management figures were to be provided to the bank on a quarterly basis.
- Debenture figures to be provided monthly.
- Fire and Accident insurance cover to be arranged.
- Key person Insurance cover to be arranged on the joint lives of the Managing Directors for five years at £250,000 each, with the policy assigned to the Bank.
- A Deed of Priority to be established, whereby the Bank would rank in priority to the extent of £300,000 over the company's assets.

Part Two - June 1989 to February 1990

Operational Problems
The growth, resulting from the take over of Scottish Trailers, meant that HRT has focused most of its energies on achieving sales. This has caused serious operational problems. HRT has not paid enough attention to the throughput of the customized sales orders once they have been won. In addition to this, the provision of financial information has been poor and quarterly management accounts have not been provided on time - a condition of the Bank's agreement. June figures arrived late but did not raise any real concerns. The September figures were not provided until early December. No action was taken on the basis of these figures.

HRT has achieved a fast growth in turnover but has suffered from the failure of administration to keep up with sales. A particular problem has been late delivery. The company has introduced a new order-monitoring system aimed at assisting the reduction of the order backlog and improving production planning. By the end of January, the company was operating near its overdraft limit. A cheque presented for £60,000 took the overdraft into excess by almost this amount.

The Bank took the following initial action - Contact made with HRT to find out why the cash flow excess? HRT advised that the extra cheques going through the account right now are for stocks of a different trailer, the "Mega" trailer. This trailer is being sold to existing and new customers as an alternative and is expected to improve sales growth. Sorry about the excess on the account but it's only a temporary blip.

When asked about the cheque for £60,000, Lyn Black explained that the cheque is a deposit payable to solicitors for the purchase of a disused factory which it is planned will accommodate all the company's operations. The factory is planned eventually to accommodate all the company's trailer adaptation, distribution, administration and training needs. The acquisition price is low at £600,000 compared with an open-market value in excess of £1m. The factory is being acquired from a local authority at such a good price because the authority needs to raise finance quickly in order to avoid being charge capped. The funds for the purchase are to come from the subordinated loan from Sun UK Ltd. which has been increased to £600,000, indicating that Sun are happy with the purpose of the loan. Sun UK Ltd. will take a charge over the factory.

The Bank concluded that at this stage the decline in the liquidity surplus was due to substantial capital expenditure and operational problems associated with the company's rapid growth causing cash flow problems. The result was a steady rise in the amount of the overdraft facility being used, such that the cheque for the deposit on the factory has taken the overdraft considerably over its limit to £351,748.

The purchase of the freehold of the disused factory is intended to enable the transfer of all operations to this site over the next twelve months. Any surplus space will be let off on short-term lets for business start-ups.

The Bank at this stage considered that there were two options:

- Return the cheque and establish if and when funds are available from Sun UK Ltd. Returning the cheque puts the Bank in a stronger negotiating position when the meeting with the customer to review the situation takes place.
- Pay the cheque and demand immediate and satisfactory answers as to why

the company has exceeded its limit and organize a meeting.

In either case the company must provide a full, up-to-date breakdown of the current position with respect to debtors, creditors and details of stock held and work in progress. The company had not been fully open with the Bank about the factory purchase. Although this could provide the solution to the pressing space problems and appears to have been purchased at a good price, it again shows a lack of financial planning and control. The operational problems are a very disturbing feature which make it likely that the overdraft has become fully utilized

The excess on the overdraft was allowed, subject to confirmation of the involvement of Sun UK Ltd., the production of a copy of the contract for the factory purchase, a full plan detailing the cost implications of the move and debenture figures confirming the debtor cover available. In addition, faced with the delays in the provision of financial information, the company's Accountants were asked to carry out a survey of HRT's debtor book.

The situation is to be reviewed in June 1990, taking into account the Accountants report, by which time some improvement would be expected to the cashflow position.

Part Three - March 1990 to June 1990

On the completion of the factory purchase, the excess on the overdraft was paid off and the overdraft limit of £300,000 was not exceeded again. However, there was still concern about the cash flow position and the Accountants were asked to report on the debtor book.

Further Developments
The next set of management accounts received in June, representing the year-end accounts, demonstrated sales more or less on target. However, gross profit margins were significantly down resulting in a trading loss. HRT, faced with falling sales of its basic product, had not reduced its workforce but instead entered a new and complementary market providing service networks. It does not have direct experience with providing networks but, instead, has recruited additional "key staff" to meet these contracts.

HRT has been experiencing some problems on these contract debtors. The company has been finding out the hard way that networks are difficult to get right first time. Debtors in the Management Accounts as at the end of April 1990 were £2.16m. indicating substantial funds available once the production and delivery problems are resolved. The directors estimate that, as at the beginning of June 1990, debtors have grown to around £3m.

As a result of the delivery problems and the continuing impetus to reach higher sales targets, the company has relaxed the policy of taking large deposits with "customization" orders. The overdraft position has shown no sign of improvement and HRT is operating consistently at the limit.

The Accountant's Report
The Accountant's survey of the debtor book reveals:

a) There is reservation of title on the stocks of Sun Trailers and additional components (Romalpa clause) but it does not relate to debtors' monies. This is despite assurances from the directors, when the original facilities were agreed, that no Romalpa clause was in force and there was no indication of such a clause on the invoices HRT receives.

b) Faced with sales falling off on its "Dimensions" machine, the company has recently entered into 'service' contracts for the supply of the "Mega" Trailers. These contracts are not simple sale contracts but entail:

- The supply of "Mega" machines
- The final check of machines at the customer's site.
- The guarantee that the Trailers will run fault-free for a specified period.
- A continuing obligation to service.

Customers are:
- Using the retention as an excuse to hold on to their cash as long as possible.
- Being extra cautious, holding on to the retention until they are completely satisfied.
- Making counter-claims and disputing the final contract figure.

After considering the impact of Romalpa on the debtor book, eligible debtors are worth £450,000.

Debtors - Accounting Practice
The company has followed an accounting practice of treating confirmed orders as actual sales when a deposit of 40% or more of the total pro-forma invoice is taken. The directors have made a rough estimate that only 10% of the debtor figure applies to goods completed and awaiting collection. Hence, the debtor figure is virtually all for goods not yet completed and does not apply to trade

debtors in its normal usage. The monies due are balance payments on contracts placed on which work may not have been started. The directors have stated that the sales which are cancelled and lost due to delivery problems are when the deposit taken is less than 40%. However, where there have been severe delivery delays, the company has been forced to give discounts to those customers who paid a deposit of 40% or over. An estimated profit is taken into account before the units are manufactured and delivered to the customer. The debtors outstanding figure represents profits from contracts not yet fulfilled by the company. As debtors include a profit element on unfulfilled contracts, the net profit should be reduced by the net profit margin on these debtors. The Bank is in a vulnerable position by relying on the debtors within the security position. The debenture is weakened considerably due to:

- The nature of the debtor book.
- The stock being subject to **Romalpa**.
- The charge which Sun UK Ltd. has on the factory premises.

In Conclusion

Many of the existing problems still remain:

- Financial control and cash flow planning is still weak.
- The product mix is questionable.
- The involvement of Sun UK Ltd. is still putting pressure on the company regarding the stock flotation.
- There is total reliance on one supplier.
- Provision of management figures and information is late.

The relationship now between the Bank and the Company has been strained and in the future the company must undertake more careful cash flow planning and control if the business is to prosper and meet the ultimate ambitions of both the Directors and Sun UK Ltd:

- Provision of management figures to include management accounts, debenture figures, budget and cashflow actuals to compare with forecasts.
- Debtor analysis to include a breakdown to show deposits received, debtors for contracts started but not yet completed, normal trade debtors and an aged debtor list.
- Creditor analysis to include identification of preferential creditors and aged list of creditors.

- Full stock analysis. This should take into account the fact that a high proportion of the stock is customized machines which are very difficult to value and probably have a very low re-sale value. In addition, unless the work done on customized machines is covered by a contract, there may well be disputes with regard to the work done leading to non- or part-payment only.
- Sun UK Ltd could be approached, as they are major funders of the business, to explore the possibility of their providing additional *cash flow* support.

Postscript:
Sun UK Ltd decided that the best approach would be to take a closer involvement in the cash management of the business with the result that the bank accounts were transferred to Sun UK Ltd's bankers.

IN CONCLUSION

*In this chapter from the two case studies reviewed, sales targets, liquidity and the resulting monthly cash flows must be scrutinized to monitor the performance of the business whether it is large or small. If projections show the company can manage its cash flows each month and this deviates, then the reasons why should be investigated urgently. Such a change may well be an **early warning sign** of future problems. The maintenance of good practices and rapport with both the lender and the equity provider is essential for the progressive development of any business, be it large or small.*

5
CASH FLOW AND RESTRUCTURING

Corporate and debt restructuring can be necessary for a variety of reasons. It can be driven by the company directors, shareholders or external creditors or any combination of stakeholders involved in the corporate structure. Turnaround situations are very varied and could be for example:

- Low return on capital for type of business
- Cash crisis
- Stagnant business - often in mature industries
- Growth orientated, but growing too fast!
- Extraordinary write-off or extraordinary loss
- Several years of successively lower profits

Management can endeavour to redress all the problems; but a number of studies have revealed that using an external person or persons can bring a focus that Management may find hard to achieve themselves.

An American 18-month study of sick companies at the Frank Hawkins Kenan Institute of Private Enterprise at the University of North Carolina took place reviewing what consultants can do to diagnose corporate ills and suggest cures. They concluded that a business which is in decline needs competent professional advice from an impartial consultant, who is familiar with the entire turnaround process. The study team interviewed more than 80 US nationally known turnaround managers, reviewed some 600 articles, and analysed 300 case studies.

The paramount problem is not seeing trouble ahead until it becomes intractable.

Business failure begins with early signals of decline, which are often unobserved or ignored. Many businesses that are in decline are not aware of it, because their management has not noticed either the internal or external signals of decline. Research confirms the requirement that - especially in near-turnaround circumstances - it is critical to pay attention to those internal and external elements affecting the success of a business. Internal elements - including the basic business functions - are most easily controlled by management, though, paradoxically, often poorly controlled. External elements - considered to be uncontrollable - include legal, political, cultural, social, competitive, economic, geographical, and technological factors. Each of these can influence a business and each sends distinct signals of prospective change which may signal decline for a business. Some businesses survive the changes whereas others fail. The difference is attributable to planning based on understanding the particular signals of decline.

Watch for Early Warning Signals

Both the internal and external elements exhibit early warning signals which predict business decline. The most common warning signals that the turnaround consultant uses to analyse the extent of external elements are:

- Measures of economic growth, which give management an indication as to economic climate, influencing expansion plans;
- Credit availability and money market activity, which indicate trends in commercial and investment banking in relation to financial needs of a business;
- Capital market activity, giving a clear signal to management of the attitude of investors toward a given industry, and which signals the investment community's belief regarding the business climate;
- Business demographics, which can alert management as to the numbers of businesses entering and leaving a given industry, and which can be used as an indicator of the expansion or contraction of the market and competitive size of the industry;
- Price level changes, indicating the rate of inflation, which influence consumption and therefore have an impact on production;
- Changes in the competitive structure of the marketplace, affecting products, pricing, marketing, and distribution;
- Changing technology, whereby rapid breakthroughs and changes in products, production, marketing, and distribution are possible;

- Cultural and social changes, which can alter consumer preferences or conditions under which a product can be sold;
- Legal and political changes, such that a market can be adversely affected, thereby impacting production, sale, or distribution of a product.

The turnaround consultant who recognizes such external signals must be able to draft a turnaround plan which addresses their consequences. The planning process is more than plotting a course around the external elements; it is a course chartered for profitability despite the new obstacles. Many businesses have strategic plans that become useless because they are not adaptable to changing external conditions.

The internal elements of finance, management, marketing, and distribution may be, or may just seem to be, easier to examine. Finance, production, marketing, and distribution are those elements most frequently used as levers by turnaround consultants. Management is the force that drives these functions, and yet management is often at the root of business failures.

The internal elements are dynamic, and yet research indicates that when decline occurs there is a lack of control over them. Decline does not happen overnight; rather it occurs in stages. The early decline stage is the first indication of trouble. Profits are decreasing but management does not analyse the possible causes. The profit decrease is perceived as a temporary phenomenon which will be self-correcting. Reductions continue until profits disappear. In mid-term decline, losses increase and management becomes concerned. Causes for decline are discussed and some actions may be taken. In the event that action is not taken, the business slides into late decline. Here, losses erode capital reserves. Cashflow is negative and management is scurrying to prevent collapse of the business.

Early decline is signalled by the following developments, typically by several at a time:
- Shortage of cash for meeting current obligations;
- Current assets decreasing concurrent with current liabilities increasing, reducing working capital;
- Increase in accounts payable aging;
- Increase in accounts receivable aging;
- Return on investment decreasing by 20 to 30 percent;
- Lack of sales growth;
- Several quarters of losses;
- Quarters of losses exceeding those of profits (either in dollars or number) over the preceding year or two;

- Employee absenteeism and accidents up;
- Increase in customer complaints regarding product quality, delivery, backorders, stock-outs, or service;
- Late financial and management information.

Mid-term decline is signalled by these developments:

- Inventory increasing and sales decreasing;
- Financial margins eroding, as revenue decreases and expenses continue to increase;
- Advances from banks increasing in dollar amount and frequency;
- Financial and management information unreliable, as well as late;
- Customer confidence declining and the customer base noticeably eroding;
- Vendors demanding payment on delinquent accounts and placing the business on a cash basis;
- Bank overdrafts become a form of interim financing;
- Paying accounts delayed by opportunistic customers;
- Loan covenants violated and compliance with all loan covenants demanded by banks;
- Bank borrowing more frequently used to cover payroll;
- Interest rates on indebtedness increased by banks, owing to increased risk.

By the time of late decline, the following is going on:

- Profit decreases ignored by management and attempts to raise cash;
- Attempts made to reduce operating costs, without analyzing the causes of business problem;
- Overdrawn bank accounts becoming permanent loans;
- Cash crisis;
- Accounts payable 60 to 90 days late;
- Accounts receivable 90+ days late;
- Further decline in sales owing to loss of customer confidence;
- Employee morale extremely low;
- Company credibility eroded;
- Inventory turnover excessively up, with inventory supply down;
- Suppliers requiring payment prior to delivery;
- Fewer reports issued to the bank;

- Auditors qualifying their opinion of latter;
- Cheques returned because of insufficient funds;
- Further decrease in financial margins, indicating imminent bankruptcy;
- Further cashflow negatives;
- Increase in uncollectable receivables as customers find new suppliers;
- Management team trying to convince lenders that company is viable and that liquidation or bankruptcy is not called for.

The turnaround consultant is willing not only save the business from further decline but return it to profitability. To accomplish this, the turnaround consultant must be able to restore credibility in the shortest possible time, relying, at least initially, upon a sound turnaround plan plus outstanding credentials. To have a fair chance for success, stakeholders must be convinced that the turnaround plan is viable and can be implemented.

The US study national survey reveals that fewer than 20 percent of business failures were caused by external elements. The other 80 percent are caused by the failure of management to control the internal elements. A UK study national survey revealed that 67 percent were attributable to defects in management ability. Consequently, the turnaround consultant must be able to build a team to manage the business, not only through its decline and return to profitability, but also after the consultant leaves, presumably through a period of business growth. The successful turnaround team consists of people to work with every part of the business. Among other things, they need to see to the dismissal of non-productive employees. Obsolete inventory, uncollectable receivables, inaccurately valued assets, and warranty reserves may be restated. The stakeholders must be provided with an accurate description of the business. Once accuracy is established, then reconstruction can commence.

One part of a corporate restructuring involves the flow of information and analysis of the customer. Products and markets are analysed to determine relative profitability. Those generating losses are being terminated. Saving position in the market is essential. A turnaround will be short-lived if the market is no longer available when restructuring is completed. Too often, people think of a turnaround as only reducing inventory, eliminating excess employees, delaying payables, collecting receivables, selling excess assets, cutting costs, and in effect generating cash. These procedures can be worthless, however, if they destroy the business's market position.

During turnaround, a firm's most basic methods of doing business are changed. Turnaround is a hands-on process, with the turnaround consultant steering all of the functions. Research indicates that in successful turnarounds revised budgets are created from the bottom up and accountability is strictly enforced. Actual costs are used in place of standard costing, and product contribution margins are used to determine those products which contribute the most to the fixed costs of the business. ***Analyses of cash flow are used continually*** to aid in developing (and revising) an operating plan for the business. The time frame generated and the amount of cash inflow will determine how – and how likely – the business can survive.

Reviewing accounts receivable is a critical cash flow task of the turnaround person. Classification of customers and aging of accounts receivable will indicate which customers are profitable. The business may have many customers it cannot afford to carry any longer; these are the ones who are continually delinquent in paying their accounts. The business also may have customers who pay on a timely basis but that provide little business. These should be analysed to determine whether they should be pursued for additional orders.

Banks, vendors, customers, employees, boards of directors, and others affected by the decline of a business need to be made part of the solution. Research shows that by the time they notice that a problem exists, the situation typically is approaching crisis proportions. Banks and boards tend to be balance sheet and income statement driven, and a healthy appearing balance sheet and income statement can disguise many problems. Banks and boards rarely visit the business and review operations, walk through the plant floor, and talk with employees. Mostly, they do not investigate basic financial data such as accounts receivable and payable. They tend to learn of conditions regarding employee morale, customer service, equipment condition, and other on-site conditions mainly from management.

Trade creditors are the business's lifeline to its supplies. When payments to them are delinquent, the business is in jeopardy. Management will argue that other suppliers can be obtained, but unless and until the underlying problem causing the delinquent payments is addressed, the reservoir of suppliers will evaporate, along with the company's credit. New suppliers require credit references, and changing suppliers bears a substantial switching cost. The new supplier has to produce or acquire the supplies requested, schedule delivery, and obtain payment. As the business adds new suppliers, the bank will receive credit report requests and may interpret this as a signal of decline.

Employee participation is essential in the turnaround process, whether management personnel or factory workers. Their work life and private life can be affected by the turnaround process. During turnaround, it may be essential to ask for pay concessions, for example. Hours of work and working conditions can be at stake. When employees participate in planning (or are at least consulted) as to how a business is to be restructured, they more readily tend to accept painful concessions. After restructuring a business certainly is indebted to these people, and they should be recompensed.

The US study also verifies that a business in decline tends to forsake customer service. Accordingly, one of the first steps by the consultant is to sample customer satisfaction through personal contact with some. How much rebuilding of the business by way of satisfying its customers will be determined.

Most turnarounds require some form of re-pricing strategy. Pricing affects the cash flow of the business and, accordingly, the success of the turnaround. When customer service and product quality are high, customer satisfaction also is high. Then, customer loyalty can be re-established on a non-price basis. Subsequently, in the event that prices need to be increased, it is easier for the customer to accept the increase. During most turnarounds, the level of customer satisfaction is low. Deliveries are late, product quality deteriorates, and back orders are delayed. Customer interviews will provide ample insights as to areas for improvement. And of course, the turnaround consultant must consider how much the level of customer service can be raised, given the usual cash constraints of the business.

Though often overlooked by management, numerous financial ratios have a high predictive power for the turnaround consultant. The most commonly used financial ratios were:

- Working capital to total assets,
- Retained earnings to total assets,
- EBIT (earning before interest and taxes) to total assets,
- Market value of equity to book value of debt,
- Sales to total assets.

These ratios are especially useful when applied over a time period of at least three years, which allows for establishment of patterns from which deviations can be readily discerned. A deviation serves as a red flag to identify the reason.

In reviewing the prior three years' performance, a moving analysis of the ratios can be useful. This process allows the turnaround consultant to maintain an ongoing analysis of financial trends. Once established, the procedure should be adopted by operating management. The ratios used by turnaround managers are designed to indicate ability of the business to survive. They will be of interest to investors and lenders.

A turnaround is a sustained positive change in the performance of a business to obtain a desired result; it also is the process by which a business with inadequate performance is analysed and changed to a desired result. A successful turnaround prior to a crisis avoids any form of crisis management, which is the extreme case, resulting generally in removal of top management and restructuring of financial, operational, and strategic aspects of the business.

Working with management in a turnaround, analysis and action are almost simultaneous for the consultant. The immediate requirement is to find the major problems, analyse them, and implement solutions. To help accomplish this the turnaround consultant relies on the management remaining after whatever initial purge of incompetent managers has occurred. Both groups are identified during initial analysis of a company, which may take anywhere from three days to four weeks, depending upon the size of the company and the extent of its problems.

The turnaround consultant usually works with the CEO, provided that the CEO can become part of a permanent solution. A CEO unable to assist in resolving the problems must be replaced and, in that event, the replacement is the turnaround consultant. Afterwards, a permanent CEO can be sought. The new CEO should be made part of the turnaround team as quickly as possible, providing the turnaround consultant with the opportunity to educate the CEO regarding the causes of the business's difficulties and the implementation of the turnaround plan. The other, remaining, management people round out the turnaround team. Utilizing existing management and focusing their energies and talents is less expensive than bringing in a crisis or turnaround team or hiring entirely new management. Furthermore, salvaging existing management leaves an experienced, competent team in place to manage the business when the turnaround is over and it is time for the turnaround manager to leave.

Important as it is, profitability is not really the primary mission of a business; survival is. Once survival is assured, a business' mission is to create something of value that is desired in the marketplace - it is creation of value that generates profits. Thus, preservation of the market during turnaround is essential.

Research indicates that turnaround strategies can take several forms and that the turnaround consultant must match turnaround methodologies to turnaround strategy. A turnaround can be strategic when the business needs to be redefined, e.g., changing markets and products. An operational turnaround is centred at changing operational characteristics, as through cost-cutting, generating new revenues, reducing assets. Commonly turnarounds are mounted on several fronts.

For a turnaround consultant to be effective he must have the confidence of the board of directors (and a majority of shareholders) and the authority to act. As progress is made, the turnaround consultant will gradually gain the confidence of senior management, employees, and other stakeholders. The ability to act without being encumbered by committees and boards helps the consultant to return the business to profitability.

Turnaround stategies identified in the US and UK studies include the following:

US COMPANIES	UK COMPANIES
• Revenue Generation	• Restructuring Leadership
• Product/Market Refocussing	• Cost Reduction
• Cost Cutting	• Asset Redeployment
• Asset Reduction	• Product/Market Repositioning
• Combination of the above	

Knowing which approach to use and when to use it largely determines turnaround success. It may be for example that, initially, cost cutting is required, superseded later by additional revenue generation.

In the short run, a turnaround plan can and should supersede a business's long-range strategic plan. However, once a turnaround is complete, the strategic planning process should be reinstated. Creation of a "living" strategic plan is essential to ongoing success of the business. Not all turnaround consultants agree on the time that should be allotted to implementing a turnaround plan. In general there are five stages in a turnaround:

1. Evaluation of the situation
2. Creating a plan
3. Implementation of the plan
4. Stabilization of the business
5. Return to growth of the business

In formulating the business plan the process can be to:

- Identify the *principal initiatives* required to execute the turnaround
- Look *realistically* at the timescales involved
- Develop a profit & loss account and cash flow *forecast* encompassing the above
- Consider the *immediate cash needs* and effects on the balance sheet

Debt Structuring

For the larger corporate borrower or for loan transactions – such as infrastructure projects or large corporate finance transactions – there are many instances where loan syndication will be the preferred route. Projections in terms of profitability and the resultant cash flows will be central to these deals. Sensitivity analysis will be undertaken by both the sponsors and the debt participators.

A syndicated loan is where two or more institutions combine in their efforts to extend a loan to a borrower. This can be achieved by:

- The borrower contracting with the lenders directly, with the loan administered by a common agent and using common documentation; or
- The borrower contracting directly with one lender who subsequently sells all or part of his interest in the loan to other lenders.

Syndicated lending represents a hybrid area within general commercial bank lending and has, in the main centres of operation, developed a culture and language of its own. The highly competitive nature and working relationships between the various participants in the market has led to an efficient and flexible market, where large financings can be raised by high credit quality borrowers.

US dollars have been used in London and other offshore markets for decades to finance international trade. This form of offshore financing becoming generically known as Eurodollar financing to distinguish it as offshore (as opposed to onshore US domestic dollar financing). In 1958 the dollar became convertible. Non-US residents could then hold dollar balances and the main European currencies became fully convertible into dollars. Continuing regulation of the US domestic loan market to protect the US balance of payments acted as a further incentive in the development of the offshore activity

International banking, and the syndicated loans market as we currently know it, had its origins in the 1960s. The development of the cross-border interbank market allowed lenders to come together to participate in dollar loans with a common funding basis and on common terms and conditions. At the same time, the practice of offering a floating rate developed to accommodate borrowers' desires for longer terms as an alternative to a fixed rate loan. The most common mechanism being used to define the periodic rate of interest being by reference to LIBOR (London InterBank Offered Rate)

The next development was to develop a system that priced an individual borrower's credit risk by reference to the spread over LIBOR. Finally the market developed to the point where syndicated loans became available in other currencies and indeed available within one facility in a variety of currencies. Today the syndicated loan market is one of the largest and most flexible sources of loan capital.

There are a number of alternative markets for floating rate finance as follows:

- *Commercial paper (CP)* – Corporates issue short-term paper directly to investors; this requires a back-up liquidity line of credit.

- *Medium-term notes (MTNs)* – Eurobonds are issued by corporates and others with maturities ranging from 5 to 15 years. They are expensive to issue in the gap between CP and MTNs due to the large up-front costs of issue.
- *Synthetics* – A composite product created by issuing a fixed interest bond and then swapping the fixed payments into floating rate liabilities.

Syndicated Loan Features

Price	Borrowers of appropriate credit quality can obtain funds from the syndicated loans market at a competitive cost to other forms of debt instrument
Speed	The process can take from one week to three months depending on the size and nature of the transaction
Size	Billions of dollars or other currencies can be raised in one transaction in the syndicated loan market
Administrative Simplicity	One common set of documentation is used by all the lenders involved
Confidentiality	Because of the private nature of the transaction, and the duty of confidentiality the bank owes its customer, a syndicated loan facility can be kept entirely confidential from the market if required, in contrast tapping the Eurobond market requires a public issue of debt instruments with the attendant prospectus.
Complexity	The syndicated loan can be tailored precisely to the requirements of the borrower in every detail. Every syndicated loan represents a unique facility

Type of Borrower

There are three main types of borrower, corporates, sovereigns (which includes quasi-sovereign and supranational borrowers) and financial institutions. They borrow for the following main purposes:

- Core borrowing needs

- Project financings (power stations, bridges, etc.)
- Asset financing (ships, oil rigs, etc.)
- Acquisition financing
- Balance of payment financings (sovereigns)

Types of syndicated loan facilities
There a numerous forms of syndicated loan. The main types are explained below. All syndicated loans are floating rate loans, usually linked to LIBOR. If a borrower wishes to fix the rate of interest or change the currency of a loan, a hybrid transaction can be entered into in conjunction with, or separately to, the loan where it is combined with a swap or other instrument to achieve the final desired outcome.

Term loan — A term loan is in most respects the same as a typical bilateral bank loan with a specific amount of money being borrowed for a fixed period. Drawdown can be in a single amount or in tranches within a fixed availability period. Repayment may be in instalments (known as an amortizing term loan) or as a single "bullet" repayment at the end of the loan. Amounts repaid or prepaid earlier may not be redrawn. A "balloon" repayment is the final repayment of an amortizing loan which is substantially larger than earlier instalments.

Revolving Credit Facility — A revolving credit facility (also known as a revolver) is similar to a term loan but offers the additional option to repay and redraw the facility at any time during its term, or for an initial agreed period. Usually these facilities are repayable in full at the end of the term (a bullet repayment), although reducing facilities are occasionally entered into.

Standby Facility — When short-term interest rates are lower than medium- and long-term rates it makes sense for large borrowers to raise most of their debt in the short-term markets. They typically do this by issuing Commercial Paper. CP is a corporate short-term, promissory note issued on a discount to yield basis and sold to institutional and corporate investors. It has a maximum maturity of 270 days, although most paper is issued for periods of not more than 30 days. It is a CP market requirement that all issuers of CP have in place a standby facility so that in the event they are unable to roll-over their CP for any reason funds are available to redeem the CP already in issue.

The facility is constructed in a similar way to a revolving credit, however it differs in that it is expected that the borrower will not use the facility for funding but keep it as a form of insurance, or standby. The documentation typically specifies particular events of default, which if they arise, permit banks to decline the advance of any further funds. It is also known as a backstop or swingline facility

Transferable Loan Facility A mechanism allowing banks to transfer their interest in a syndicated loan is included in the loan agreement, usually by allowing for the creation of transferable loan instruments or certificates. The prior notification or approval of the borrower is typically required.

Multi Currency Loan A multi currency loan may incorporate a multi currency option offering the borrower the opportunity to draw in a variety of currencies or switch currencies. The loan documentation contains additional clauses, to protect the lender from fluctuations in the currency of drawing compared to the base currency. In the event of default there is a similar clause allowing for compensation in respect of differences in the amount of a judgement in one currency and the amounts outstanding in another currency.

Bidding Facilities The bidding facility was an additional element added to a standby loan. A tender panel is created, the members of which tender for the short-term paper periodically issued by the borrower, the effect of this in times of adequate liquidity being to drive down further the cost of funds to the borrower.

This style of financing developed strongly during the 1980s, spawning a variety of types of standby facility incorporating different tender panel arrangements, the principal acronyms for which are shown below:

RUF   Revolving underwriting facility
MOF   Multi option facility
NIF   Note issuance facility
BONUS Borrowers option for notes and underwritten standby structures

Acceptance Credit Facilities This facility provides for the acceptance and discount of trade related bills of exchange. The lenders receive a fee for acceptance and levy a discount on the face value of the bill to reflect the current interest rate if the bill is discounted. Typically there is a six-month limit on the duration of individual acceptances.

Mezzanine Finance Facilities Mezzanine finance is a form of capital used primarily in highly leveraged transactions (HLTs) which are typically leveraged buy-outs (LBOs). It ranks behind senior debt but ahead of equity in a winding up situation, the return required by mezzanine providers being higher than that on senior debt due to the higher risk associated with mezzanine.

The provision of mezzanine finance will typically require an inter-creditor agreement to spell out the relative priorities of the different types of finance provider. This deals with such things as the extent to which senior lenders enjoy priority of access to cash flow for interest service and priority over security. It also deals with issues such as whether principal can be repaid on mezzanine finance (attractive to the borrower because it is more expensive to service than senior debt) while there is still senior debt principal outstanding.

Evergreen Facility An evergreen loan is a loan which is of indefinite duration, typically having a term of three to five years which is rolled over annually unless either party gives notice to the contrary. The triggering of the notice period is a key aspect of such agreements. Who has the option to give notice, or does it happen automatically in the absence of some notification, are key features.

There are three main geographic centres which dominate syndicated loans activity: London, New York and Hong Kong. Typical practice in respect of the detailed structuring of the loan and the method of syndication varies according to local custom. For example, in the American market it is usual for the lead bank to contract the whole of the loan with the borrower and then syndicate it. In London usual practice is to syndicate the loan before contracting with the customer, after obtaining a mandate to do so.

Other debt products, as alternatives to syndicated loans

Private Placement - It is interesting to note that when Glaxo raised the finance for the acquisition of the Wellcome group, it did so by entering into a series of £900 million bilateral loans with nine banks to raise £8.1 billion – the largest facility ever seen in the UK. Presumably it chose this course to maintain confidentiality. The bankers knew only that a large acquisition was likely and were only told of the identity of the target on the Friday before the announcement of the bid on the following Monday. So private placement of debt remains a powerful competitor to the syndicated loan facility.

Fixed Bond Issues - Whereas funds can be raised at very competitive margins, the transaction typically involves a public issue and significant up-front fees, making this market more economic for longer term borrowings. If variable rate funds are required an associated swap transaction is also necessary.

Floating Rate Notes - These are medium-term debt securities whose interest payments "float" with short-term interest rates. First issued by Citicorp in the United States in 1974, by the mid-1980s $43 billion of FRN's were outstanding.

Medium-Term Notes came into existence in the in the early 1980s to fill the gap between short-term debt markets (such as the CP market) and the bond market, which was typically used for issues having a maturity of between 5 to 15 years.

Leasing is increasingly used by asset intensive businesses as it represents a competitive source of funds. Its attractiveness is driven by the attractive tax benefits available to the capital provider, which in turn subsidises the interest rate offered.

Convertible Bond or a Bond with Equity Warrants are attractive to some issuers because the conversion right lowers the coupon on the bond compared to a straight and the conversion rights are usually pitched so that the bond will convert to equity in the future, in the absence of unforeseen hazards, so removing the need for capital repayment of the bond.

The treasurer acting for the corporate will constantly be assessing the most flexible and low-cost debt financing option for his employer. It is important therefore to understand the relative attractiveness of the syndicated loans market when compared to the other sources of debt finance when structuring the debt.

Turnaround Methodology

The least methodological aspect of a turnaround is psychological in nature. The turnaround manager has to be an autocrat, one whose instincts and skills guide the business through its difficulties. Though autocracy could have been part of the initial business problem, the turnaround manager's autocracy is necessary, albeit temporary.

The ability to deal with many problems and people simultaneously and under pressure is a skill developed by the turnaround consultant over a long period of time. Rapidly developing an understanding of the abilities of the employees and being able to mould them into a team is essential. Knowing how to negotiate with bankers, lawyers, vendors, and other stakeholders is one of the key elements of success, whereby, in effect, needed bridge capital can be obtained.

Deciding when to use an external consultant can be a difficult decision and choosing a turnaround consultant is not easy, although there are many who are prepared to take on turnaround assignments.

Laura Ashley Case Study: Part 2

In the previous book we looked at the problems facing the business during the late 1980s. We arrived at the point where the group had successfully refinanced itself due to the deal struck between Sir Bernard Ashley, who was then Laura Ashley's chairman and Takuya Okada, then Chairman of Laura Ashley's large Japanese joint-venture partner.

This deal took place in Tokyo 17 August 1990 and its result was that Laura Ashley's borrowings had been reduced significantly from £50 million to £38.7 million and therefore bringing about a resulting saving in annual interest costs. Gearing also fell from 122% to 34%.

This capital investment was seen to give the group a more flexible credit facility and management were confident that they could then embark on a significant cost reduction exercise in September.

Ref. Extel Financial Ltd (1992):
The results for year ending 26 January 1991 was a turnover of £327.5 million, compared with £296.6 million in the previous year. A loss before tax of £6.67 million, compared with the year before when the group lost £4.653 million.
Although balance sheet of business much improved, according to the Chairman's comments on these figures the depression in the UK housing market restricted growth in sales of home furnishings. Garment sales started well, but then levelled out.
Margins cut by heavy discounting by retail stores in America even though sales had grown.
Sales in continental Europe rose by 19%.
Big expansion of perfume sales by 173% in USA, South America and other new markets.
Sales in Japan rose by 88% with stores increasing to 37 from 24.

McCarthy information Ltd/*Financial Times* 18/7/91:
Mr. James Maxmin chosen as group's new chief executive.
According to the FT '... the balance sheet has already been sanitized with last year's disposal's and an injection of capital from Jusco of Japan ... but much more will be needed to turn last year's 2.6p loss per share into earnings which justify the current market price of 71p'.
'Mr. Maxmin is a marketing man who can doubtless do great things with the Laura Ashley brand name'.
'... to prevent debt rising sharply again the way forward seems to be through licensing.'

'... the risks are increased by the need to reposition the brand for the younger customer.'

McCarthy Information Ltd Sept 91:
' "More professional management techniques will generate a ton more cash," said the American-born Mr. Maxmin who was presenting a set of figures that applied to the half year before he arrived.
Pre-tax profit improved to £528,000 in the six months to July 27.'
'... Interest costs greatly reduced at £1.4million (£7m)'
'... Before Mr. Maxmin arrived, Laura Ashley's prospects were revived by ... 1,500 job losses ... seven factory closures ... sale of non-core businesses ... and a £30m cash injection from the Aeon Group of Japan..'
According to the article Mr. Maxmin said a task force was reviewing overheads in UK, Continent and in North America. He saw the group as being far too complex.
He envisaged capital investment to upgrade systmes such as tills, bar coding and stock location.
Only 22% of its goods now made in Ashley plants. 25-30% coming from other UK suppliers.

McCarthy Info. Sept 91/*Daily Telegraph* 27/9/91:
' "The Laura Ashley brand appeals to between 4p.c. and 6p.c. of the population – that is not something we want to apologise for but what we want to exploit."
According to article sales fell by 12% in Britain and trading was equally difficult in America. Japan the only exception.

McCarthy/*The Independent* 27/9/91:
Mr. Maxmin quoted as saying that the group has too many managers involved in too many tasks and that some functions were duplicated. He warned of job losses among senior and middle management.

McCarthy info/*The Times* 4/10/91:
Maxmin announced 100 redundancies among managers and support staff in a restructuring that will cost about £5 million.
All senior executives to spend a day every two months working in a Laura Ashley shop and shop staff to be given incentives to increase profitability.
Andrew Higginson, who joined as finance director in May 1990, involved in programme of cost cutting and selling peripheral businesses.
'He is unashamedly managing the business for cash.'
The group is budgeting for no upturn in sales this year and although Maxmin

states that brand has not lost any of its strength, apparently others feel its image has lost its clarity.

Mr. Maxmin intends to keep its core floral designs which make up 30% of its fashion range and to make the rest of the range a 'bit more whacky'.

The group is going to spend £10 million over the next two years on global computer systems that will allow the merchandise department to stock stores with products that will sell. Pricing and positioning will be evaluated.

McCathy Information Ltd/*The Evening Standard* 22/9/94:
According to this article the Chairman, Hugh Blakeway Webb, announced that shareholders should only expect a nominal dividend once again due to restructuring costs and a patchy recovery in its major markets.

The group has paid out £3.3 million in exceptional restructuirng costs, including controversial payoff of former chief executive Jim Maxmin costing £1.2 m as well as elimination of a number of other management jobs.

Only the sale of interest in Revman industries helped push profits up to £5.1 million in the 26 weeks ending July.

Geoff Haslehurst appointed new finance director since the departure of Andrew Higginson in July.

No acting Chief Executive at this time.

Financial Times 23/8/97:
The article contrasts the difference between the Company's fortunes around the time of its flotation in 1985 before which it had been experiencing compound pre-tax profits growth of 48% and now with further losses and very low share price.

Chief Executive - Ann Iverson warned that the Company would lose money in the first half year. Several of her appointees had already left the group.

The share price is almost 60% below its launch price.

Investment Research of Cambridge suggest that the fall in the share price will continue. They state that Companies that depend on consumer fashions are vulnerable and that it has been hard for Laura Ashley to change direction from its association with a vanished countryside.

Family company's are often badly run. The Ashley family was probably not demanding enough of its Welsh factory workers, as modern retailers are of their suppliers.

The FT states that back in 1990 the Ashley management were trying to reorganize its supply lines to provide the right goods in its shops at the right time and in the right quantities and Ann Iverson repeated the same thing this week.

Cash Flow and Restructuring

***Financial Times* 20/8/97:**
Talks about yesterday's first half loss warnings and the fact that it has occurred after a highly promising start made by Ann Iverson who inherited a Company that had made a loss of £31 million in 1995, but who 10 months into her arrival announced that dividend payments would be made for the first time since 1989 and a return to profit for 1996.

She also announced an ambitious expansion programme in the US and UK. When the share price doubled in a year and the interim results where available last September Iverson announced that the strategy was 'right on track'.

Unfortunately, seven months later this did not seem to be the case.

The expansion into the US had come unstuck. The smaller sites had been swapped for larger ones and the stock ordered to fill these stores had not sold sufficiently, leaving the group with warehouses full of merchandise.

In the article a Laura Ashley senior manager explains that the expansion into the US overestimated the strength of the brand and that resources put into place were insufficient to cope with their plans.

The programme is to be frozen until store sales improve and a £2 million advertisement campaign is to be introduced to support this.

Ann Iverson explained that the infrastructure caused the plans to fail.

Apparently, other observers see the problems in reality to be those that it has had since the late 80s – updating its image and supplying the products the market wants.

A rival retailer states that Next and Oasis are the fashion for younger women and for older women its classic labels such as Gucci, Ralph Lauren and Chanel. The Chairman of Laura Ashley, John Thornton, sees a big market opportunity in the 35-50 year-old age group, which makes up 45% of the female population and which is only catered for by 9% of stores.

***Financial Times* 19/11/97:**
The non-executive directors, including Sir Bernard Ashley, 35% stakeholder, asked for Ms. Ann Iverson's resignation. She will depart immediately.

This has been brought about by the fact that Company has announced three profit warnings this year and pre-tax losses of 4.5m in September.

Jim Walsh, finance director, who will be replaced as soon as replacement found. David Hoare replaces her, who was drafted in as chief operating officer, after last profit warning in September.

Iverson will leave with payment of her basic salary of £450,000.

Mr. Walsh will receive £300,000.

Analysts are expecting the group to incur a loss of £10million this year.

Financial Times **16/1/98**:
Can the company doctor David Hoare cut the £25million annual losses and keep the company within its £67million borrowing limit.
Action taken so far is sale of Welsh factories and cut in stocks, but remaining problem is whether the North American business can be turned around, if not the exit costs could threaten the group's survival.
The article states that fresh financing would allow more rapid rebuilding of the brand.
After severing of links with manufacturing the share price fell nearly 25% to 26 pence.
In North America, total and like-for-like sales fell by 13% in the two months to January 10.

Financial Times **6/3/98**:
Laura Ashley is to receive £8 million for a 13% share in Laura Ashley, Japan. Share price at 37pence.
A Malaysian conglomerate, Malaysian United Industries, said it would inject 43.7m net of new equity into Laura Ashley, taking 40 % of the enlarged capital.

Financial Times **10/6/98**:
Sir Bernard Ashley resigns from board as non-executive director, to be replaced by his son Nicholas.
This resignation comes after the cash injection of £43.7million in April which rescued the ailing company. Sir Bernard Ashley's stake is now only 20%.
Motoya Okada also replaces his father Takuya Okada as representative of the interests of Jusco, the Japanese partner.

The Times **13/8/98**:
David Hoare leaving after 9 months in job, being replaced by his deputy Victoria Egan, who formerly headed a retailing company within MUI.
Richard Pennycook, finance director, who joined in March is also going.
John Thornton to stay as chairman but board will be dominated by executives from MUI.
20% of head office staff is planned to be removed saving about £3million a year.
Nicholas Ashley remaining a non-executive director.
Full year losses are expected to be £17million before exceptional costs. Sales are well down, but trading at a discount is also lower.

***The Financial Times* 2/10/98:**
Laura Ashley; the struggling retailer said yesterday that sales are continuing to plummet and that shareholders will have to wait for up to five years for a turnround ...

This is where we are at the time of writing – let us hope that Victoria Egan – the new CEO can fix it this time !!

In Conclusion

Within this chapter we looked at a variety of reasons where corporate and debt restructuring can be necessary together with a series of turnaround consultant methodologies.

We then examined debt structuring in terms of loan syndication and other alternative debt products. The next chapter features a further case study incorporating more of the issues reviewed.

6

CASE STUDY - THE CANADIAN ALUMINIUM COMPANY

This case looks at cash flow and debt restructuring. It features an aluminium production company. It is recommended that readers study the debt restructuring request and, in particular, the cash flows projections. With the high levels of debt relative to equity in this type of project, cash will be a key issue in the payment of equity returns and loan repayments.

The prospective Bank has developed a good relationship with the Syndicate Lead Bank over the last year and has now been asked to consider taking part in a syndicated loan facility. The Canadian Aluminium Company has a sound market reputation and an established track record. The deal is that the prospective Bank has been asked to contribute $20m to the syndicate. Sections of the prospectus have been abridged to reduce the volume of paperwork.

Readers should note particularly the cash flow statements on page 176 indicating the feasibility of the debt repayment, but dependent, of course, on the operational cash flows. As you read the case, you will note the strong ownership structure and the fixed contractual arrangement for the off-take of the high-quality aluminium being produced. Also, the plant has secure power sources and spare capacity in terms of output efficiencies. CANALCO also benefits from a strong market position and good labour relations.

Information Memorandum

The information in this memorandum has been provided by Canada Aluminium Company (CANALCO) or extracted from published sources. CANALCO has authorized The Canada Bank Limited (the "Arranger") to arrange the facility described in this memorandum (the "Facility"), has approved this memorandum, and has requested and authorized the Arranger to distribute it on its behalf to potential participants in the Facility.

CANALCO has confirmed to the Arranger that (1) the information in this memorandum is true, complete and accurate in all material respects at its date, (2) the opinions, projections and forecasts in it and the assumptions on which they are based were arrived at after due and careful consideration and enquiry and genuinely represent its view and (3) there are no material facts or circumstances which are not disclosed in this memorandum and which could make any of such information, opinions, projects, forecasts or assumptions untrue, incomplete, inaccurate or misleading in any material respect or which, if disclosed, might reasonably be expected adversely to affect the decision of a person considering whether to provide finance to it.

The Arranger has not independently verified the contents of this memorandum. No representation, warranty or undertaking (express or implied) is made, and no responsibility is accepted by the Arranger as to the adequacy, accuracy, completeness or reasonableness of this memorandum or any further information, notice or other document at any time supplied in connection with the Facility.

The sole purpose of this memorandum is to provide background information to assist the recipient in obtaining a general understanding of the business of CANALCO and its outlook. It is not intended to provide the basis of any credit or any other evaluation and is not to be considered as a recommendation by the Arrangers that any recipient of this memorandum participate in the Facility. Each recipient of this memorandum contemplating participating in the Facility must make (and will be deemed to have made) its own independent investigation and appraisal of the business, financial condition, prospects, creditworthiness, status and affairs of CANALCO or anyone else.

The delivery of this memorandum at any time does not imply that the information in it is correct as of any time after its date, or that there has been no change in the business, financial condition, prospects, creditworthiness, status or affairs of CANALCO or anyone else since that date.

The Arranger does not undertake to assess or keep under review the business, financial condition, prospects, creditworthiness, status or affairs of CANALCO or any other person now or at any time during the life of the Facility or (except as specifically provided in the Facility documentation) to provide any recipient or participant in the Facility with any information relating to CANALCO or otherwise.

The distribution or possession of this memorandum in or from certain jurisdictions may be restricted in law. Persons into whose possession this memorandum comes are required by CANALCO and the Arranger to inform themselves about and to observe any such restrictions. Neither CANALCO nor the Arranger accepts any liability to any person in relation to the distribution or possession of this memorandum in or from any jurisdiction.

CANADA ALUMINIUM COMPANY

The Canada Bank Limited has been mandated to arrange a medium-term loan facility by Canada Aluminium Company - CANALCO - on a fully underwritten basis. We are pleased to invite your institution to join this transaction on the following principal terms.

Borrower:	Canada Aluminium Company.
Facility Type:	Underwritten US dollar term loan ("the Facility").
Purpose:	Refinancing of existing debt.
Amount:	US$50,000,000 (fifty million US dollars).
Security:	(a) Unconditional undertaking from the Government of Canada under the advance payment provisions of the Quota Agreement. (b) Assignment of rights and benefits of the Borrower under the Quota Agreement.
Final Maturity:	Five years from the date of signing of the Facility Agreement ("Signing").
Interest:	LIBOR (being the average of the rates at which the Reference Banks are offering to prime banks in the London Interbank Market one-, three-

Case Study: The Canadian Aluminium Company

	or six-month US dollar deposits, rounded upwards to the nearest 1/16th per cent) plus a margin of 0.60 per cent per annum.
Commitment Commission:	Nil. (Drawdown will take place immediately following Signing.)
Fees:	The following fees will be payable:

Status	Amount	Fee
Lead Manager	$10 million	0.25%
Co-Lead Manager	$7.5 million	0.20%
Manager	$5.0 million	0.15%
Participant	$2.5 million	0.10%

The fee will be payable on the amount allocated and calculated at the rate appropriate to the amount committed.

Interest Periods:	Three or six months at the option of the Borrower.
Interest and Fee Calculations:	All interest and per annum fees shall be calculated using a year of 360 days and the actual number of days elapsed.
Drawdown:	The Facility shall be drawn down in one amount immediately following Signing.
Repayment:	The Facility shall be fully repaid in a single instalment at Final Maturity.
Prepayment:	Prepayment of the whole or any portion of the Facility is permitted without premium or penalty, subject to the giving to the Agent of 30 days' prior written notice. Prepayments may be made on interest payment dates only, in minimum amounts of US$10,000,000 (ten million US dollars) and integral multiples thereof. Amounts prepaid cannot be re-borrowed.

Reference Banks:	Three banks representative of the Lending Banks to be selected by the Agent.
Taxes:	All payments under the Facility will be made free and clear of all present and future taxes (including stamp taxes), levies, imposts, duties, charges, deductions, liabilities and withholdings ("Taxes") whatsoever.
	In the event that any Taxes are, or become, payable, payments under the Facility shall be grossed up accordingly and the Borrower shall pay the Taxes and forward to the Agent official tax receipts evidencing payment of the Taxes within 30 days of their due dates.
Documentation:	A facility agreement ("the Facility Agreement") in form and substance acceptable to all parties incorporating, *inter alia*, the following clauses:

- Unconditional undertaking from the Government of Canada under the advance payment provisions of the Quota Agreement
- Assignment of Quota Agreement with the Government of Canada
- Representations and warranties repeated throughout life of Facility
- Alternative interest rates
- Increased costs
- Provision of Accounts and other financial information reasonably required by lenders
- Full transferability
- Material adverse change
- Waiver of sovereign immunity
- Pari passu ranking of the Facility
- Negative pledge
- Events of default including cross-default
- Maintenance of 51% ownership by Canada Government

	Acknowledgement from Canada Government that the Facility will be treated as Qualifying Debt. Such documentation will be further subject to the approval of any relevant authorities.
Governing Law and Jurisdiction:	The Facility Agreement shall be governed by and construed in accordance with English law and shall be subject to the non-exclusive jurisdiction of the courts of England.
Agent:	The Canada Bank Limited
Arranger:	The Canada Bank Limited

The Arranger reserves the right to close the books at any time, increase the Facility in the event of over-subscription and allocate participations at its sole discretion.

We look forward to working with your institution in this transaction, and would greatly appreciate your earliest response, but in any event not later than Monday 19 December 1994.

THE BORROWER

General Information

Name of the Company:	Canada Aluminium Company (The "Company" or "CANALCO")
Registered Office and Location of the Company's Plant:	Plot No 150 Road No 94 Area No 948 State of Canada
Postal Address:	PO Box 570, Calgary
Telephone:	830000
Telefax:	830083
Telex:	8253 CANALCO BN
Commercial Registration:	999
Bankers:	Calgary Commercial Bank Bank of Canada Citibank NA

	National Bank of Canada
	Standard Chartered Bank
Auditors:	Ernst & Young
	PO Box 140
	Calgary
	State of Canada

History and Nature of Business
CANALCO was incorporated as a Canada Shareholding Company (closed) in 1968 to construct, own and operate a primary aluminium smelter. Commercial production commenced in 1971. CANALCO has its own combined cycle gas and steam turbine power plant based on locally available natural gas. There have been no significant interruptions since inception.

CANALCO's product mix is geared towards producing high-quality ingots and semi-processed aluminium which sells at a premium to the LME cash settlement price on international markets. As a benchmark CANALCO produces ingots with a minimum purity level of 99.7 per cent. CANALCO has recently been awarded 150 9002 certificate for the quality of its products.

Ownership
CANALCO's ownership structure is as follows:-

The Government of Canada	77%
The Canada Public Investment Fund	20%
Simplon Investments Limited	3%
Total	100%

The Government of Canada
The Government of the State of Canada has been the primary promoter of CANALCO.

Canada Public Investment Fund (CPIF)
The Canada Public Investments Fund was established in Canada by a Royal Decree in 1971. The purpose of CPIF, as stipulated by Article 2 of the Law of the Public Investments Fund, is for financing investments in productive projects of commercial nature, which belong to the Canada Government or its agencies that offer industrial loans, or to general organizations, whether such projects are executed by these agencies and organizations alone or with the participation of private companies. Financing of such projects is carried out by means of

loans or guarantees. In all such financing operations, conditions and situations specified by the Administrative Board of CPIF are applied and complied with."

The affairs of CPIF are supervized by an Administrative Board composed of the following:-

- Chairman - the Minister of Finance and National Economy
- Two members of the Council of Ministers to be nominated by the President of the Council of Ministers
- Chairman of the Central Planning Commission
- Governor of the Canada Monetary Agency.

The Administrative Board reports directly to the Council of Ministers, to whom a detailed annual report is submitted outlining CPIF's operations and its financial status. CPIF does not publicly disclose financial information. The Administrative Board can also propose funds to be allocated annually in the General Government Budget for financing CPIF.

CPIF has been particularly active in financing petrochemical and heavy industry projects in Canada It has participated in all of the initial financing of the Canada Basic Industries Corp. (CABIC) projects.

Simplon Investments Limited

Simplon Investments Limited (SI) was incorporated in 1969 in Hamilton, Bermuda by Edward Simplon of Germany and a UK company, Bloy Ltd., to serve as a holding company of shares held in CANALCO. Founded in 1876, Edward Simplon is a private company which produces a wide variety of metal powders and pigments in various locations in Europe and overseas, and markets these products worldwide.

Since 1974 SI has acted as a marketing company for its share in the production of CANALCO. In 1987, Simplon Investments Limited (Canada) was set up as a wholly owned subsidiary of SI, taking over all the marketing and trading activities of its parent company.

Organisation and Management

CANALCO is managed by a seven-member Board of Directors headed by Jack Shaw, who is the Chairman of the Company. Four of the Directors are nominated by the Canadian Government, two are nominated by CPIF and one is nominated by SI. The Board of Directors is primarily responsible for formulating the policies and business strategies of the company.

The operational activities of the company are the responsibility of its Chief Executive, Mr. Gudvin K Tofte, and Deputy Chief Executive, Mr. A K Saunders.

The company has six main divisions: Administration, Finance, Metal Production, Maintenance, Carbon and Metal Services, and Engineering and Power.

Board of Directors of the Company

Nominees of the Government — *Examples of other positions held*

Jack Shaw
Chairman
Minister of Development & Industry

Hermin Kanter
Deputy Chairman
Minister of Commerce & Agriculture

Sharon Mason
Director
Under-secretary, Ministry of Development & Industry

Mr. Raymond Smith

Director
Assistant Under-secretary for Economic Affairs,
Ministry of Finance & National Economy

Nominees of CPIF

Henry Abbots
Minister of Electricity & Industry - Canada Arabia

Director

Mr. Isaac Smith
Director
Vice President & Managing Director CABIC

Nominees of SI

Mr. Gert Robins
Director
Director of Simplon Investments Limited

Present Facilities

CANALCO's present facilities comprise:

(i) Four production lines for production of primary aluminium with a rated capacity of 460,000 tonnes per annum. CANALCO was built initially with a capacity of 120,000 tpa, which was increased gradually over the years to 205,000 tpa by 1991. CANALCO subsequently implemented an expansion programme costing US dollars 1.4 billion, which involved the addition of a fourth reduction line (Line 4). Line 4, with a rated capacity of 235,000 tpa, was commissioned one month ahead of schedule in May 1992. Simultaneously the older reduction lines were modernized by July 1994 (the Retrofit programme). This increased the capacity of the older lines by 20,000 tpa to 225,000, thereby taking the overall capacity of the company to 460,000 tpa.

(ii) Three gas-fired power stations with a total generating capacity of 1350 MW, including an 800 MW, combined cycle power plant. The installed power-generating capacity is more than sufficient to meet CANALCO's requirement of 800 MW to run its plant and associated facilities.

(iii) CANALCO sells 250 MW of power to the State electricity grid through a power link established for the purpose. The tariff payable by the Canadian Government enables CANALCO to recover the cost of generation, the capital investment incurred to establish the linkage with the State electricity grid and related financial charges.

(iv) The Carbon Department, where the anode materials are mixed, pressed and baked.

(v) The Marine Terminal, through which alumina and other raw materials are imported.

(vi) The Casthouse, where molten aluminium is cast into finished products.

Product Mix

CANALCO is geared to the production of standard ingots of a minimum purity of 99.7 per cent. A breakdown of 1993 production is set out below:

	Tonnes per annum
Standard Ingot	220,351
Billet	107,882
Rolling Slab	58,220
Liquid Metal	53,863
T-Ingots	6.550
Other	68
Total Finished Metal	446,934

CANALCO's facilities allow flexibility in the product mix to meet market requirements.

The prolonged slump in the prices for primary aluminium induced the leading producers in the West to enter into a Memorandum of Understanding and introduce production cutbacks. In cooperation with this move to improve prices, CANALCO voluntarily reduced its production by 20,000 tpa. With considerable improvement in the prices for primary aluminium of late, CANALCO is constantly monitoring the production cutback.

Alumina Supply
Alumina supplies are sourced from Western Australia under long-term contracts, which are renewable at the end of 1999. The Company enjoys a long-standing relationship with its suppliers and is confident that the supply contracts will be renewed.

Gas Supply
Natural gas used by CANALCO is largely a by-product of oil drilling. CANALCO has secured its power source under a long-term contract with the Canada National Oil Company (CANOCO), valid until 2004. CANOCO is wholly-owned and controlled by Canadian Government.

Off-take Arrangements
CANALCO operates only as a production facility and does not have the responsibility of selling the aluminium it produces. The responsibility rests with CANALCO's shareholders. In the case of the Government and CPIF, their share of aluminium produced is marketed through Canada Aluminium Marketing Company Ltd (CAMCO). SI's share of aluminium produced is used primarily to meet aluminium requirements of SI's associated companies.

The off-take of aluminium from CANALCO by its shareholders is governed by the 1990 Quota Agreement. As described under "Security Arrangements", this Agreement requires each shareholder to purchase aluminium, subject to certain purity specifications, in proportion to their shareholding in CANALCO and to pay a metal price which meets CANALCO's total net cash requirements.

Marketing of Aluminium
The major shareholders (the Government and CPIF) are responsible for stocking and marketing 97 per cent. of CANALCO's production. This responsibility is carried out by CAMCO, which functions as the marketing arm of CANALCO. CAMCO was founded in 1976 to handle the sale and stock control of the Government's share of production.

CAMCO has proved to be an effective marketing organization, establishing relationships with over 50 major customers in 26 countries. In addition, CAMCO has developed considerable expertise in hedging against fluctuations in aluminium prices and foreign currency exposure. The creation of a separate marketing company has enabled CANALCO to concentrate on physical production, as reflected in its high purity standards and high level of environmental protection.

Although CAMCO is responsible for the overall marketing of the product, CAMCO and CANALCO work closely together to identify and fulfil customer requirements.

Current Markets

CAMCO has particularly concentrated its efforts to meet the demand from the growing economies of the Far East and the Middle East. The following table shows the geographical distribution of export sales:

CAMCO Sales per cent.

	1989	1990	1991	1992	1993
Middle East	65	65	66	63	39
Far East	16	13	4	27	52
Europe	5	6	5	4	4
ISC/SEA*/Others	14	16	5	6	5

* Indian sub-continent/South East Asia

During 1993, CAMCO sold about 127,163 mt in Canada, 35,095 mt to Arabia and 9,583 mt to Malaysia. Almost all export sales are on a long-term contract basis, by which precise tonnages are fixed annually and prices negotiated quarterly.

From 1994 onwards CAMCO's annual share of CANALCO smelter production is 446,000 tonnes of primary aluminium with the following available capacities:

- 120,000 mt in billet form (will reach about 200,000 mt by 1996)
- 100,000 mt in slab form
- 50,000 mt in wheel alloys form
- 40,000 mt in T-ingot form

The balance is liquid and commercial grade ingots.

Risks and Alleviating Factors

The major risks faced by an aluminium producer relate to the price of aluminium in world markets and the supply and pricing of its primary inputs, alumina and energy.

In CANALCO's case, these major risks are mitigated to a significant extent because CANALCO operates only as a production facility for its shareholders and has the benefits of the 1991 Quota Agreement. Under the 1990 Quota Agreement CANALCO undertakes to sell, and the other organizations each undertake to buy their Quota Percentages of the total quantity of aluminium produced by it at a price that will enable CANALCO to recover its net cash out-goings (inclusive of amounts needed to service principal and interest on debt pertaining to CANALCO's plant). This arrangement insulates CANALCO from the price risk associated with the world aluminium markets.

With regard to the risks relating to the supply and pricing of primary inputs, that is alumina and energy, CANALCO is protected through long-term supply agreements. Considerable reliance is placed on shipping lines for input of alumina.

In relation to energy supply, as mentioned above CANALCO has an installed generating capacity of 1350 MW, which is far in excess of its requirement of 800 MW.

On labour relations, CANALCO has had a strike-free record over the last two decades. This record is expected to be maintained.

CANALCO enjoys an enviable industrial safety record. CANALCO is well covered, through appropriate insurance policies, against all types of customary risks including property damage, machinery breakdown, business interruption and shipping risks.

Financial Performance

Under the terms of the 1990 Quota Agreement, all of the company's aluminium production is transferred to the shareholders at transfer prices, set by the Board of Directors, to recover on a continuing basis the company's net cash outgoings including all capital expenditure, loan repayments and associated financial charges.

The shareholders independently market their respective quotas of production. Any margin between the sale price, net of selling and distribution costs, and the transfer price achieved by the shareholders is not reflected in CANALCO's financial statements. Consequently, the "net surplus for the year" (as shown in the historical financial statements that follow) does not reflect the profits accruing to CANALCO's shareholders through the sale of aluminium.

APPENDIX 1

Security Arrangements

Security for certain creditors of CANALCO is provided through an assignment of CANALCO's rights and benefits under the 1990 Quota Agreement (which covers, *inter alia*, the obligations of CANALCO's shareholders to purchase CANALCO's total production of aluminium and the obligations of the Government to make certain advance payments equal to the amount of any debt including interest owed by CANALCO to such creditors which is due but unpaid) to the Law Debenture Trust Corporation (Cayman) Limited – the Security Trustee.

Some of the key aspects of the security arrangements are summarized below:

The 1990 Quota Agreement

Obligation to Purchase Aluminium

Under the 1990 Quota Agreement, CANALCO undertakes to sell and the Government, CPIF and SI (the "Purchasers") each undertake to buy, their Quota Percentage of the total quantity of aluminium produced by CANALCO. The Quota Percentages for the Purchasers are:

Canadian Government	77 percent.
CPIF	20 per cent.
SI	3 per cent.

The Purchasers are not required to take aluminium which is of a purity less than 99.7 per cent. (or, if less than 99.7 per cent. but more than 99.5 per cent., which has impurities above certain specified levels).

The price paid by the Purchasers to CANALCO for the aluminium varies in order to enable CANALCO to recover its net cash outgoings (inclusive of debt service pertaining to CANALCO's plant). Such price is determined from time to time by CANALCO's Board of Directors in accordance with the provisions of the 1990 Quota Agreement (and may be adjusted by any premium or discount for non-standard specifications).

Each Purchaser's obligations to purchase aluminium from CANALCO under the 1990 Quota Agreement extends until the earlier of: (i) the termination of the 1990 Quota Agreement by agreement between CANALCO and such Purchaser; (ii) the winding up of CANALCO and; (iii) the termination of the 1990 Quota Agreement in relation to such Purchaser by giving 6 months notice expiring after 1 January 2005.

CANALCO's right to terminate (or agree any amendment to) the 1990 Quota Agreement is assigned to the Security Trustee.

Advance Payments

The Government undertakes to pay to CANALCO from time to time on demand by CANALCO a sum equal to the aggregate of any and every amount of Qualifying Debt (as defined below) which is then due from CANALCO but not paid in full. However, the Government is not obliged to make such an advanced payment in respect of any amount of Qualifying Debt originally scheduled to mature on a specified date until the earlier of (i) such specified date, (ii) the failure by the Government to pay any sums due from it under the 1990 Quota Agreement and (iii) the failure by the Government to perform any of its other obligations under the 1990 Quota Agreement if such failure is not remedied within 30 days.

Each amount demanded of the Government by CANALCO in respect of any outstanding amount of Qualifying Debt will constitute a debt due to CANALCO in the amount demanded and must be paid by the Government in accordance with the terms and provisions of the 1990 Quota Agreement and notwithstanding CANALCO's failure to produce or sell aluminium for any reason whatsoever (including, for example, the closure or destruction of CANALCO's plant or CANALCO's insolvency). The Government's obligation to make advance payments in respect of Qualifying Debt continues for the term of the 1990 Quota Agreement (which is of an unlimited duration). The Government has undertaken in the Acknowledgement not to terminate the 1990 Quota Agreement without the consent of the Security Trustee.

Qualifying Debt

Qualifying Debt is that indebtedness of CANALCO incurred under an agreement or instruments which is (or are) specified in a notice (a "Qualifying Debt Notice") signed by CANALCO and approved by the Government and acknowledged by the Security Trustee.

Assignment and Transfer of 1990 Quota Agreement and the Government's Acknowledgement

All of CANALCO's rights under the 1990 Quota Agreement are assigned to the Security Trustee pursuant to the assignment (the "Assignment"). The rights assigned include the right to make demands and receive amounts due under the 1990 Quota Agreement. CANALCO is entitled to exercise its rights under the 1990 Quota Agreement until such time as the Agent gives notice to the contrary. However, CANALCO is required to direct that all amounts due as advance payments from the Government are paid directly to the Trust Account specified by the Security Trustee.

The Security Trustee agrees that it will not give the notice referred to above until 10 days after an Enforcement Event (and then only if the Enforcement Event is continuing), except in the case of an Enforcement event which itself incorporates a 30-day grace period.

Enforcement Events are any of the following events:

(i)   CANALCO's failure to perform any of its obligation under the 1990 Quota Agreement or the Assignment and such failure is not remedied within 30 days; or

(ii)   The Government's failure to pay any sums due from it under the 1990 Quota Agreement or fails to perform any or its other obligations under such agreement and such failure is not remedied within 30 days; or

(iii) Any Qualifying Debt not being paid when due.

CANALCO has given notice of the Assignment to the other parties to the 1990 Quota Agreement. The Government, in its Acknowledgement of the Assignment has, *inter alia*, undertaken not to agree to any amendment, cancellation or termination of the 1990 Quota Agreement without the Security Trustee's consent.

Security Trust Deed
Pursuant to the Security Trust Deed, the Security Trustee holds the rights and benefits assigned to it pursuant to the Assignment for the benefit of the beneficiaries thereof. The Beneficiaries are the holders of qualifying Debt (and their Representatives) who have complied with the requirements of the Security Trust Deed. These requirements include the submission by the Beneficiaries to the Security Trustee of a Qualifying Debt Notice for such debt and an instrument (a "Designating Instrument") designating such debt as Qualifying Debt. Provided that the Security Trustee has no knowledge or notice of an Enforcement Event, the Security Trustee is required to execute such Designating Instrument, whereupon the indebtedness of CANALCO therein referred to will become Qualifying Debt for the purposes of the Security Trust Deed and the Beneficiaries named in such Designating Instrument will have the benefit of the security held thereunder on the same terms and conditions as all other Beneficiaries.

The Security Trust Deed provides for certain procedures to be followed on the occurrence of an Enforcement Event including, *inter alia*, procedures for the meetings of Beneficiaries and the enforcement of the security held by the Security Trustee. Following the receipt or recovery of any proceeds arising from the enforcement of the security, the Security Trustee is required to distribute such proceeds on a pro rata basis to the Beneficiaries after reimbursing itself for its own costs and expenses.

Only the representatives of the holders of Qualifying Debt are entitled to give notices and directions to the Security Trustee under the Security Trust Deed; individual creditors are not entitled to require the Security Trustee to take any action or proceeding thereunder.

Law and Jurisdiction
The 1990 Quota Agreement is governed by the laws of Canada, and the Assignment and the Acknowledgement are each governed by the laws of England.

The parties to each of the 1990 Quota Agreement, the Assignment and the Acknowledgement submit to the jurisdiction of the courts of England and courts of Canada.

Lenders' Security
The Loan will be designated as Qualifying Debt by way of a Qualifying Debt Notice to be signed by CANALCO and the Government on or about the date on which the Loan Agreement is signed. Such Qualifying Debt Notice will be submitted to the Security Trustee together with a Designating Instrument conforming to the Qualifying Debt Notice and the requirements of the Security Trust Deed. Upon execution of such Designating Instrument by the Security Trustee, the Lenders and the Agent, as their Representative, will become Beneficiaries of the security held by the Security Trustee under the Security Trust Deed.

Case Study: The Canadian Aluminium Company

STATEMENT OF INCOME AND RETAINED EARNINGS
Year ended 27 December, 1993

	Note	1993 US$'000	1992
Statement of income			
Sales		520,455	329,287
Premia less discount		5,997	6,556
		526,452	335,843
Cost of sales		381,279	271,496
Gross surplus		145,173	64,347
Expenses			
General and administration		1,914	2,122
Financial charges	15	71,170	28,952
Depreciation	3	56,660	19,008
Amortization of deferred charges	4	9,271	2,503
Provisions of kilns' rebuild	14	2,622	3,292
		141,637	55,877
Surplus for the year		3,536	8,470
Statment of retained earnings			
Balance at beginning of year		152,710	144,394
Surplus for year		3,536	8,470
Transfer from Line 4 equity	10	383	-
		156,629	152,864
Transfer to statutory reserve	11	35,905	-
Transfer to capital reserve	12	91	114
Directors' fees		40	40
		36,036	154
Balance at end of year		120,593	152,710

STATEMENT OF CASH FLOW
Year ended 27 December, 1993

	1993	1992
	US$'000	
Bank balances and cash at beginning of year	8,372	17,300
Cash received from shareholders	528,146	333,984
Cash available to meet net cash flows	536,518	351,284
Operating activities		
Cash paid to suppliers and employees	(412,239)	(291,912)
Financial charges	(63,931)	(27,569)
Director's fees paid	(40)	(40)
Cash flow - operating activities	(476,210)	(319,521)
Financing activities		
Line 4 equity	-	25,864
Proceeds from long-term borrowings	237,462	620,154
Repayment of long-term borrowings	(53,777)	(15,388)
Cash flow – financing activities	183,685	630,630
Investing activities		
Payment towards property, plant and equipment	(187,047)	(616,364)
Proceeds from sale of plant and equipment	123	245
Financial charges	(17,931)	(37,902)
Cash flow – investing activities	(204,855)	(654,021)
Net cash outflows for year	(497,380)	(342,912)
Bank balances and cash at end of year	39,138	8,372

Case Study: The Canadian Aluminium Company

NOTES TO THE 1993 FINANCIAL STATEMENTS

1. **Activities**
   The company is a Canada Joint Stock Company (closed). It owns and operates a primary aluminium smelter.

2. **Significant Accounting Policies**
   The financial statements have been prepared in conformity with the Canadian Commercial Companies Law and in accordance with international Accounting Standards. The significant policies adopted are as follows:

   (a) *Accounting convention*
   The financial statements are prepared under the historical cost convention.

   (b) *Depreciation and amortization*
   Freehold land and assets in process of completion are not depreciated. The cost of other property, plant and equipment is depreciated by equal annual instalments over the estimated useful lives of the assets. Pre-production and production development costs, being treated as deferred charges, are amortized over the estimated periods of benefit. Depreciation and amortization charges, where applicable, commence from the start of the year following the completion of installation or acquisition of the assets.

   (c) *Inventories*
   Raw materials are stated at cost, which is determined on an average basis. Work in process is stated at production cost, calculated on an average basis, and includes an appropriate proportion of overheads. Stores stock is stated at cost, which is calculated on a first-in first-out basis after making due allowance for any obsolete items.

   (d) *Employees' terminal benefits*
   The company has made provision for amounts payable under the Canada labour law and company benefit schemes applicable to all employees' accumulated periods of service at the balance sheet date.

   (e) *Income*
   Sales
   Sales represent the amounts invoiced to the shareholders during the year in respect of aluminium produced, at a predetermined transfer price approved by the Board.

Premiums less discount
This represents the addition to or deduction from the amounts invoiced to the shareholders resulting from the additional costs incurred or savings made by the company when supplying aluminium to the shareholders in a form other than standard output.

(f) *Provision for kilns' rebuild*
A provision is made each year to spread the cost of rebuilding the kilns over their estimated useful lives. The actual cost of rebuilding the kilns is charged against the provision.

(g) *Major maintenance and repairs*
With the exception of the cost of rebuilding the kilns, all other major maintenance and repair costs are expensed as incurred.

(h) *Interest related to expansion projects*
Interest paid on loans raised in connection with the financing of expansion projects, net of interest earned on related deposits, is capitalized until the commencement of commercial production.

3. **Property, Plant and Equipment**
The estimated useful lives of the assets for the calculation of depreciation are as follows:

Freehold Buildings	45 years
Electrical generating plant	25 years
Plant, machinery and other equipment	3 to 22 years

	Freehold land and buildings	Electrical generating plant	Plant, machinery and other equipment	Assets in process of completion	Total
Cost		US$'000			
At 28 December 1992	115,163	91,750	259,952	1,418,031	1,884,902
Additions during year	2,120	330	19,259	131,295	153,040
Transfers to deferred charges	-	-	-	(166,497)	(166,497)
Transfers during year	-	255,920	683,298	(939,218)	-
Cost of Disposal	(219)	-	(2,106)	-	(2,325)
At 27 December 1993	117,064	348,000	960,439	443,617	1,869,120

Case Study: The Canadian Aluminium Company

	Freehold land and buildings	Electrical generating plant	Plant, machinery and other equipment	Assets in process of completion	Total
Depreciation					
At 28 December 1992	37,793	40,968	146,894	-	225,655
Charge for year	2,976	13,904	39,780	-	56,660
Relating to Disposals	(138)	-	(2,078)	-	280,099
At 27 December 1993	40,631	54,872	184,596	-	280,099
Net Book Accounts					
At 27 December 1993	76,433	293,128	774,843	443,617	1,589,021
At 28 December 1992	77,370	50,782	113,058	1,418,037	1,659,247

4. **Deferred Charges**

Pre-production and production development costs are amortized over twenty-three years in equal annual instalments from the year following that in which the costs were incurred.

	1993	1992
	US$'000	
Balance at beginning of year	57,937	-
Transfer during the year from property, plant & equipment in connection with:		
- 76 cell expansion	779	-
- Line 4 expansion	165,718	-
	224,434	57,937
Amortization	46,375	37,104
Balance at end of year	178,059	20,833

5. **Inventories**

	1993	1992
	US$'000	
Raw materials in transit	13,364	25,344
Stores stock in transit	2,971	2,497
Raw materials	38,670	29,614
Work-in-process	47,864	47,130
Stores stock	51,894	28,707
	154,763	133,292

6. **Accounts Receivable and Prepayments**

	1993	1992
	US$'000	
Advances to contractors - expansion projects	-	13,609
Prepaid expenses	4,962	3,367
Other receivables	2,503	2,944
	7,465	19,920

7. **Transactions with Shareholders**

   All of the company's metal production is transferred to the shareholders at transfer prices set by the Board of Directors to recover the company's net cash outgoings including all capital expenditure and loan repayments.

   The shareholders market their respective quotas of production independently. Any margin between the sales price, net of selling and distribution costs, and the transfer price achieved by the shareholders is not reflected in these financial statements.

   In the ordinary course of business, the company purchases certain supplies and services from parties related to the shareholders, principally natural gas and public utility services. A royalty payment, based on production, is made to the Canadian Government.

8. **Accounts Payable and Accruals**

	1993	1992
	US$'000	
Trade accounts payable	22,809	27,686
Accrued expenses and other payables	38,861	46,533
	61,670	74,219

9. **Share Capital**

   The authorized share capital consists of 100,000,000 ordinary shares of US$2.66 each of which 79,000,000 are issued and fully paid. (1992: 25,000,000)

10. **Line 4 Equity**

    During 1993 this was utilized to issue 54,000,000 ordinary shares of US$2.66 each. The balance has been transferred to retained earnings in accordance with a shareholders' agreement.

11. Statutory Reserve

	1993	1992
	US$'000	
Balance at the beginning of year	16,622	16,622
Transfer during year	35,905	-
Balance at end of year	52,527	16,622

As required by the Canadian Commercial Companies Law, a statutory reserve, equal to 25% of the issued share capital, has been created by transfers from retained earnings. The reserve cannot be utilized for the purpose of distribution, except in such circumstances as stipulated in the Bahrain commercial Companies Law.

12. Capital Reserve

	1993	1992
	US$'000	
Balance at the beginning of year	300	186
Transfer during year	91	114
Balance at end of year	391	300

As required by the Canadian Commercial Companies Law, an amount equal to the surplus on disposal of property, plant and equipment during the year has been transferred to the capital reserve. The reserve cannot be utilized for the purpose of distribution, except in circumstances as stipulated in the Canadian Commercial Companies Law.

13. Loan Financing

The term loans carry interest at commercial rates. All loans in connection with Line 4 expansion, ED link and the retrofit project are secured over the future production of the company.

1992		Total	Current Maturities	Drawdowns	Instalments due Between 1995-98	After 1998
	Variable Rate					
953,262	Line 4 expansion	1,016,072	87,416	15,461	549,670	394,447
92,346	Working capital Revolving credits	89,851	-	-	-	89,851
24,072	76 Cell expansion	16,420	7,652	-	8,768	-
-	ED link	70,000	12,000	-	46,798	11,202
80,000	Retrofit Ph-3	90,000	10,000	20,000	80,000	20,000
136	Albaskan	484	484	-	-	-
1,149,816		1,282,827	117,552	35,461	685,236	515,500
	Fixed Rate					
141,354	Line 4 expansion	180,287	18,801	-	83,103	78,383
-	Retrofit Ph-4	18,500	-	14,000	20,684	11,816
20,769	76 Cell expansion	14,359	6,410	-	7,949	-
1,309	Other loans	960	322	-	638	-
163,432		214,106	25,533	14,000	112,374	90,199
1,313,248	TOTAL	1,496,933	143,085	49,461	797,610	605,699
49,487	Current maturities	143,085				
1,263,761	Non-current maturities	1,353,848				

The company has arranged an interest rate swap agreement, which has the effect of fixing the rate of interest on the Line 4 expansion US$ borrowings totalling US$325,000,000 (1992: same) until the year 2000.

The current maturities of the loan financing will be financed by the shareholders through payments for the transfer of metal as the transfer prices are set by the Board of Directors to recover loan repayments as well as the company's net cash outgoings, including all capital expenditure (Note. 7).

14. Provisions for Kilns' Rebuild

	1993	1992
	US$'000	
Balance at the beginning of year	10,154	6,826
Transfer during year	2,622	3,292
Balance at end of year	12,776	10,154

15. Financial Charges

	1993	1992
	US$'000	
Loan Interest	79,431	65,883
Other Interest	122	114
	79,553	65,997
Interest earned	492	218
Exchange gains	450	809
	942	1,027
Financial charges – net	78,611	64,970
Interest capitalized during year	(7,411)	(36,047)
Exchange gains capitalized during year	-	29
Financial charges	71,170	28,952

16. Capital Commitments

Commitments for capital expenditure for projects entered into and not provided for in these financial statements are estimated at US$34,944,000 (1992: US$82,013,000) for projects authorized and contracted for. The amounts authorized, but not contracted for, are US$95,614,000 (1992: US$117,620,000).

17. Comparative Figures

Certain of the prior year amounts have been reclassified to conform with the presentation in the current year.

7
CASE STUDY: SIME DARBY
cash flow and $1 billion

This final case study looks at a large Malaysian conglomerate facing some extreme changes to the normal cash flow patterns that were seen previously over many years. We begin by reviewing an interesting press cutting of April 1995.

> **Sime Darby looks outside Asia to spread its wings -** *Financial Times* **4/95**
> The English seaside town of Bognor Regis is the somewhat unlikely setting of one of the most ambitious moves ever made by a Malaysian company. In the middle of 1994, Sime Darby, the Malaysian conglomerate which describes itself as south-east Asia's biggest multinational, bought Britain's Lec Refrigeration for £21.7m ($35m). It now plans to pump £30 m into Lec's Bognor-based operations.
>
> Mr. Nik Mohamed Nik Yaacob, Sime Darby's Chief Executive, says: "We have a substantial presence throughout south-east Asia and Australia. Now we want to spread our wings further. We aim to bring the Lec plant up to the state-of-the-art manufacturing standards and expand operations into continental Europe. Later we plan to bring the technology we are investing in back to this region and set up similar operations here."

Case Study: Sime Darby

In recent years Malaysian companies and individuals, flush with cash as a result of seven consecutive years of 8 per cent growth, have been quietly investing in property in Britain. Now Malaysia's conglomerates are eyeing other investment opportunities in the country.

Sime Darby was started in 1910 by Messrs Sime and Darby, a Scot and an Englishman. Initially it managed a 500-acre rubber estate in what was then Malaya. Over the years, it developed into one of Britain's biggest plantation companies. It also became involved in extensive trading activities and, through a franchise arrangement with the US Caterpillar group, the heavy equipment industry. In the late 1970s, Sime Darby was "Malaysianized", with the government taking a controlling share. Company headquarters were moved to Kuala Lumpur.

Until recently the group was seen as a steady, if unspectacular, performer. While other Malaysian groups regularly increased profit levels by between 20 and 30 per cent, Sime Darby trundled quietly along. Pre-tax profit for the year to June 30 1994 at M$904 m (US$366 m), a 7.5 per cent rise on the previous figure. For the six months to December 31, pre-tax profit was M£483 m, a 15 per cent advance on last time. Sime Darby's conservative image has changed as a result of recent deals. Last year, it bought out a remaining 49 per cent stake in Consolidated Plantations, its listed subsidiary, in a M£1.05 bn share swap deal. Some minority shareholders in Consolidated questioned aspects of the buyout saying their interests had been ignored. But the deal was timely. Consolidated has extensive palm oil plantations; during the last six months, palm oil prices have surged by more than 50 per cent. Sime Darby has taken a 40 per cent stake in a power scheme under Malaysia's ambitious independent power producer programme. Analysts say the project will generate substantial *cash flow* for the group in the long term.

The deal that has excited most interest has been Sime Darby's declared interest in a majority stake in United Malaysian Banking Corp, Malaysia's fourth largest bank in terms of assets. Control of UMBC will allow Sime Darby to play a significant role in Malaysia's fast expanding financial services sector. UMBC has an extensive branch network within Malaysia and overseas. It also has a merchant bank, a finance company and a stockbroker. Analysts say the likely purchase price for a proposed 60 per cent stake will be about M$750 m.

Some experts chart Sime Darby's more adventurous stance to a mid-1993 management change, when Mr. Nik Mohamed, 45, took over from Tunku Ahmad Yahaya, chief executive since the ealry 1980s and now deputy chairman. The group now comprises more than 200 companies with activities including property development, oil and gas, tyre manufacturing, leisure, paint products and latex in Malaysia and the Philippines, as well as car distribution in Hong Kong and southern China. In Malaysia, Sime Darby has some of the country's biggest housing developments and has reaped handsome rewards from an average 30 per cent per annum surge in house prices over the last three years.

It has few cash constraints. Group reserves, combined with those of Consolidated Plantations, are estimated to be at least M$1.5 bn. The main handicap to expansion is a shortage of management. Analysts say diversification has meant management might not always be fully appraised about what is going on in various units. While acquisitions, such as that of Lec, might make long-term sense, the group must ensure that it has the management resources to cope with its ambitious expansion.

Mr. Nik Mohamed admits Sime Darby has to be careful. "We will remain what people like to call a conservative group", he says. "But despite that conservatism Sime Darby has always been on the lookout for opportunities. For a long time we were called the slumbering giant, yet we have produced record profits in each of the last eight years. If that's slumbering, it's not bad at all."

Trading progress continued in terms of gross revenues, pre-tax profits and retained earnings, as shown in the following table:

Group Results as at Year End 30th June 1997

	1995 RM m	1996 RM m	1997 RM m
Gross revenue	9394.2	10779.7	13236.0
Profit before taxation	1012.3	1329.9	1683.0
Taxation	(262.9)	(402.2)	(505.3)
Profit after taxation	749.4	927.7	1177.7
Minority interests	(180.2)	(245.2)	(341.9)
Earnings for the year	569.2	682.5	835.8
Extraordinary items	(42.1)	10.1	(20.4)
Profit attributable to shareholders	527.1	692.6	815.4
Transfer to statutory reserves	-	(27.8)	(48.2)
Dividends	(323.7)	(383.9)	(384.9)
Retained profit/loss for the year	203.4	280.9	382.3

The gross revenue was analysed and detailed by sector activity, including the new "Banking" activity contribution at RM346.7 m profit in 1996 and RM494.5 m in 1997 representing 30 % of group profit before interest of RM1583.3 m, thus quickly becoming the dominant contributor.

Analysis by Activity	Gross Revenue			Profit Before Interest		
	1995 RM m	1996 RM m	1997 RM m	1995 RM m	1996 RM m	1997 RM m
Plantations	970.5	914.2	1000.8	155.2	139.5	136.9
Manufacturing	1662.8	1399.7	1524.5	120.3	92.0	109.1
Property	535.3	725.8	801.8	136.1	212.8	233.4
Heavy equipment and motor vehicle distribution	4365.1	4752.8	5727.2	333.4	311.1	434.6
Financial services	*269.3*	*1314.5*	*2560.2*	*37.1*	*346.7*	*494.5*
General trading, services and others	1855.1	1905.3	2050.2	131.4	130.5	174.8
	9658.1	11012.3	13664.7	913.5	1232.6	1583.3
Group's share of gross revenue of associated companies	(263.9)	(232.6)	(428.7)			
Group gross revenue	9394.2	10779.7	13236.0			

However, the fortunes of the Group were soon to be dramatically impacted by huge loan problems within its Financial Services division. *The Financial Times* Report of 12 November 1997 stated:

Sime Darby sees threat from Asian slowdown - *Financial Times* 12/11/97

Sime Darby, Malaysia's largest multinational conglomerate, will be affected by the expected slowdown in growth in Asia next year and by loan problems in the company's financial division.

Nik Mohamed Nik Yaacob, chief executive, acknowledged that customers of the conglomerate's stockbroking unit, Sime Securities, had lost "quite substantial amounts of money" during the recent stock market fall, but said the borrowings of these customers were fully collateralized. "These losses are covered by collateral ... If there is a debt (owed) to Sime Securities, then it will be collectable" he said.

Sime Bank, one the company's most profitable operations, will also be hit by Malaysia's financial crisis. The bank is regarded as vulnerable to the deflation of Malaysia's asset bubble, which includes easing property prices in an oversupplied market, falling share prices and a contraction in consumer spending. The bank's loan growth of 70 per cent last year was much higher than the average of nearly 30 per cent. Now that non-performing loans must be reported three months after interest payments lapse - compared with six months previously - the level of declared bad debts may rise from about 3 per cent in June this year, Mr Nik Mohamed said. "If non-performing loans go up to 12-13 per cent (next year), as industry analysts expect, it would result in a M$120 m (US$21.6 m) loss" he said; referring to the loss derived from lapsed interest payments. He was confident that M£1.93 bn in shareholders' funds would prove adequate to cover any bad debts.

The problems in the financial services arm, which contributed 30 per cent of pre-tax profits in the last financial year, will undoubtedly affect the group's overall earnings. Tractors Malaysia, the heavy equipment and motor vehicles division, which contributed 26 per cent of pre-tax profits, is also likely to be hit. Tractors Malaysia imports all its heavy machinery and cars. The sharp depreciation of the ringgit, a government campaign to cut down on heavy machinery imports, and a decision to defer several large infrastructure projects would have a clear effect on earnings, Mr Nik Mohamed said.

However, there were some grounds for optimism. The plantations division, which contributed 8 per cent of pre-tax profits, is expected to benefit from the ringgit's depreciation and the fact that relatively low rainfall in the region has helped drive up the price of palm oil, of which Malaysia is the world's largest producer.

Case Study: Sime Darby

> Mr Nik Mohamed expected the region's economic downturn to last one or two years, but added that the group would emerge from it strongly. It was studying the opportunities for expansion, possibly in finance, into Thailand and Indonesia.

The full effect on trading was subsequently shown in March 1998, when the group interim results for the half-year were published showing a loss of over RM1 bn, with the Financial Services Division making a loss of RM1.7 bn. This was the first loss shown by the group for as long as anyone can remember.

Sime Darby incurs RM1.1 bn Interim Loss – *Business Times* (Malaysia) – 9/3/98

Sime Darby reported a group pre-tax loss of RM1.1 billion for the first six months ended 31 December 1997 compared to a pre-tax profit of RM850 million in the corresponding period of the previous year.

The loss was incurred despite a 24 per cent increase in gross revenue to RM7.89 billion from RM 6.38 billion previously. Group after-tax loss was RM1.28 billion compared to group after-tax profit of RM621.1 million before. Group loss per share was 29.1 sen against earnings per share of 19.9 sen previously and an interim gross dividend of 1 sen per share less tax (5 sen last time) has been declared.

Sime Darby's core businesses in plantations and in Hong Kong (excluding banking) performed satisfactorily in the first half of the year, reporting higher profits than in the previous corresponding period. However, the results for the second half-year will be affected by the economic slowdown throughout South-East Asia and profits are expected to be somewhat lower than that for the first six months, Sime Darby said in a statement.

With the impact of Sime Bank's losses, Sime Darby group will show a loss for the full year. Sime Bank suffered a group loss of RM1.81 billion (RM1.57 billion by the bank itself) of which RM1.09 billion is attributable to Sime Darby. This arose mainly from provisions at SimeSecurities Bhd (RM713 million) and provisions against loans and investments at Sime Bank (RM917 million) necessary in the current economic climate.

Sime Darby's plantation division reported significantly higher profits on the back of higher crude palm oil prices. Its tyre manufacturing arm's sales improved due to strong demand for replacement tyres consequent to increased car sales in recent years. However, a sharp decline in sales towards the end of the six months dampened the operating results of the conglomerate's heavy equipment and motor vehicle distribution divisions. In addition, lower profits were contributed by the property division due to fewer launches and a drop in unit sales. Sime Darby's BMW and Mitsubishi operations in Hong Kong recorded strong growth with improved motor vehicle registrations. This, coupled with the effect of translating Hong Kong profits into ringgit, resulted in a 85 per cent increase compared to previous period.

Operations in Singapore achieved improved profits, but this was negated by share of losses in an associate company arising from translation of a foreign currency loan. A delay in the start of real estate operations in the Philippines resulted in a small loss before including interest income derived from its surplus funds. The marginal decline in Hastings Deering's profit was due to lower demand from the mining sector which was offset by the translation effect of the stronger Australian dollar to the ringgit.

Meanwhile, Sime Darby has requested for the continuation of suspension in the trading of its shares on the Kuala Lumpur Stock Exchange pending an announcement on the group's 60.35 per cent stake in Sime Bank.

Also, the company has appointed Mr. Martin Smith Berry, director and group finance director, while Datuk Khatijah Ahmad has been appointed a member of the company's audit and accounts committee.

Sime Darby Group - Interim Results for the half-year ended 31/12/97

	1996 RM m	1997 RM m
Gross revenue	6381.0	7890.9
(Loss)/profit before exceptional items and taxation	784.5	(1152.1)
Exceptional items	65.5	40.8
(Loss)/profit before taxation	850.0	(1111.3)
(Loss)/earnings	463.2	(676.2)
per share - sen		
(Loss)/earnings	19.9	(29.1)
Earnings excluding the results of Sime Bank	16.8	17.8
Gross dividend	5.0	1.0

Case Study: Sime Darby

Director's Review of Results

The major loss suffered by the Sime Bank group of RM1,810 million (and RM1,570 million by the bank) of which RM1,089 million is attributable to Sime Darby, arose mainly from provisions at SimeSecurities of RM713 million and provisions against loans and investments at Sime Bank of RM917 million. These provisions are necessary in the current economic climate.

The losses need to funded; and taking all the options into account, management recommended and the Board has agreed, that Sime Darby withdraw from banking. Talks are now being held to merge the bank and accept a minority position. After concluding the disposal of the majority position in the bank, the remaining Group businesses are both viable and adequately funded.

The Sime Darby Group businesses, excluding banking, have performed satisfactorily in the first half of the year, reporting higher profits than those earned in the corresponding previous period, with particularly pleasing results from Plantations and Hong Kong. However, the results for the second half year will be affected by the economic slowdown throughout South East Asia and it is expected that profits will be somewhat lower than those reported for the first half year.

With the effect of the losses in Sime Bank group, Sime Darby Group will show a loss for the full year and the Board has declared a gross interim dividend of 1.0 sen against 5.0 sen per share last year.

The breakdown of the Group's results before taxation, excluding exceptional items by the respective operating divisions/regions is as follows:

Half-year ended 31 December

	1996 RM m	1997 RM m
Plantations	74.3	107.3
Tyre manufacturing	19.3	23.0
Heavy equipment and motor vehicle distribution	80.4	77.5
Property development	81.6	75.9
Malaysia	57.5	55.4
Hong Kong	74.4	137.9
Singapore	49.5	43.0
Philippines	(0.4)	(1.7)
Australia	<u>63.6</u>	<u>64.5</u>
	500.2	582.8
Investment income	14.5	18.3
Interest (net)	<u>36.3</u>	<u>23.6</u>
	551.0	624.0
Financial services	<u>233.5</u>	<u>(1776.8)</u>
(Loss)/Profit before exceptional items and taxation	784.5	(1152.1

Sime Darby expects RM246 million loss from bank disposal - *The Star* 12/3/98

The proposed disposal by Sime Darby of its 60.35 per cent stake in Sime Bank Bhd would result in a RM246 million loss for the group, assuming that the exercise is completed by 30 June, it was announced yesterday.

Amanah Merchant Bank said in a statement on behalf of Sime Darby that based on the unaudited consolidated net tangible assets of Sime Darby as at 31 December 1997, the proposed disposal would result in the reduction of the group's net tangible asset value per share to RM2.33 from RM2.43.

Sime Darby has proposed to sell its stake in Sime Bank, held by Sime Darby Financial Services Holdings Sdn Bhd to RHB Bank Bhd. At the same time, KUB Malaysia Bhd will also sell its 30.01 per cent share in Sime Bank to RHB Bank.

Sime Darby to embark on aggressive measures to restore financial health - *The Star* 7/5/98

Conglomerate Sime Darby Bhd, which recently hived off financially troubled Sime Bank Bhd to RHB Bank, will soon embark on aggressive measures to restore the financial health of the group, said its chief executive officer Tan Sri Nik Mohd Yaacob. He said Sime Darby was now set to make its operations "lean and mean" to prepare itself to take advantage of opportunities when the economy recovered.

In an interview in Sydney recently, Nik said *"Sime Darby wants to get into a high net cash surplus position. I am looking at building up a net cash surplus of about RM1 billion, a level we were used to before"*. He said that while Sime Darby was already in a net cash position, this must be strengthened to improve its financial position. Nik expalined that many of Sime Darby's non-wholly owned subsidiaries were in a net cash position, where their borrowings were less than the cash they held. "The wholly-owned subsidiaries are, however, in a net borrowing position", he said, pointing out that if the two were merged they would more or less even or balance out. "What we are trying to do in the next two to three years is to not only increase our net cash position but also prepare ourselves for the difficult times ahead", he added.

Cash Flows

It is worth studying the group cash flows to see that, although the profit contributions from Financial Services in 1996 and 1997 were coming through strongly, behind the scenes the normal cash flow patterns of the group were changing significantly from those seen before - as reported in the annual accounts:

	1995 RM m	1996 RM m	1997 RM m
Net cash inflow from operating activities			
Operating profit	913.5	1232.6	1583.3
Adjustments for non-cash items	119.6	153.5	146.7
Operating profit before working capital changes	1033.1	1386.1	1730.0
Increase in trade debtors and other receivables	(131.7)	(420.9)	(2289.7)
Decrease/increase in inventories	(337.9)	40.0	(114.5)
Increase in trade creditors and other payables	306.7	299.2	1003.0
Decrease in banking assets	-	382.8	(7515.1)
Decrease in banking liabilities	-	(659.3)	8217.6
Net cash generated from operations	870.2	1027.9	1031.3
Taxation paid	(253.9)	(318.2)	(392.1)
Dividends from associated companies	16.0	24.7	24.4
Investment income*	47.1	38.2	33.6
Interest received*	63.4	97.8	132.0
Interest paid*	(11.7)	(38.7)	(65.9)
Net cash inflow from operating activities	731.1	831.7	763.3
Net cash outflow from investing activities	(528.9)	(1,7708.)	(2,331.4)
Net cash inflow/(outflow) from financing activities	(491.9)	1244.7	(214.3)
Net increase/(decrease) in cash and cash equivalents	(298.7)	305.6	(1782.4)
Cash and cash equivalents at beginning of the year	1285.9	985.9	1294.5
Foreign exchange differences on opening balances	(10.3)	3.0	13.1
Cash and cash equivalents at end of the year	985.9	1294.5	(474.8)

* Excluding Financial Services

Case Study: Sime Darby

Readers will note the shift from cash and cash equivalents of RM985.9 million positive in 1995 to a position of RM474.8 million negative in 1997.

At the time of writing, I await the full 1998 cash flow statement, but we can gather from the recent press articles reviewed that the resultant cash flows will be bleak and that the Group will have to work very hard to restore their former reserves.

cash is still king　　**cash is still king**

BIBLIOGRAPHY

H. I. Ansoff, *Corporate Strategy*, Penguin, 1965

F. Altman, *Corporate Bankruptcy in America*, Heath, Lexington, Mass., 1971

Edward I. Altman, 'The Success of Business Failure Prediction Models, An International Survey', *Journal of Banking and Finance* 8, 1984, PP.171-198, North-Holland

P. I. Altman, 'Financial Ratios, Discriminant Analysis and the Prediction of Corporate Bankruptcy', *Journal of Finance*, Vol.23, No.4, Sept 1968, pp 589-609

Andrews, 'The Formulation of Business Strategy', *Harvard Business Review*, 1971

J. Argenti, *Corporate Collapse: The Causes and Symptoms*, McGraw-Hill, 1976

Russ Banham, 'Dell Corporation', *CFO Magazine*, Dec 1997

A. Bathory, *The Analysis of Credit: Foundations and Development of Corporate Credit Assessment*, McGraw-Hill, 1987

W.H. Beaver, 'Financial Ratios as Predictors of Failure', *Journal of Accounting Research*, Vol. 5, pp.71-111

D.Bibeault, *Corporate Turnaround*, McGraw Hill, 1981

Boyadjian & Warren, *Risks Reading Corporate Signals*, John Wiley & Sons, 1987

Shelly Branch, 'Go with the flow - or else', *Black Enterprise*, Vol.22, No.4, Nov1991 pp.77-82

Robert Buchele, 'How to Evaluate a Firm', *California Management Review*, 1962, pp 5-16

Dianne Hayes Casey, 'Cash Flows from Operations: Why it Deserves More Attention', *Corporate Controller Journal*, Vol.4, No.6, July/Aug 1992, pp.46-48

E. I. du Pont de Nemouns, *The du Pont Formula*, 1950s

William Enderlein, 'Credit Analysis: The Power of Cash-Flow Analysis', *Commercial Lending Review*, c.1989

Financial Times 22/2/91, *Cash Flow Becomes the Determining Factor*

James M. Gahlon & Robert L. Vigeland, 'Early Warning Signs of Bankruptcy Using Cash Flow Analysis', *The Journal of Commercial Bank Lending*, Dec 1988

Bibliography

Kenneth A. Hiltz & Kristine M. Gail, 'Settling Corporate Workouts', *Business Credit Journal*, Vol. 93, No.9, Oct 1991, pp. 8-10

T. H. Jury, 'Understanding Money in Business', *FSMD*, 1989

Christopher Kemball, 'Laura Ashley's Refinancing Plan', *Acquisitions Monthly*, Dec 1990, pp.25-26

Kotler, *Stages of the Life Cycle*, 1972

John R. F. Lehane, Timothy l'Estrange & Adrian Powles, *International Financial Law Review* (UK), June 1990, pp.7-15

McKinsey & Co., *Economic Value to the Customer*, Forbus and Mehta, 1979

Manchester Business School, *Corporate Strategic Planning*, 1988

R.S. Norgard, 'The Causes of Corporate Collapse', *Australian Accountant (Australia) Journal*, Vol.57, No.3, April 1987, Pp.24-25

J. Brian O'Connell, 'How Inventory Appraisals Are Done', *The Journal of Commercial Bank Lending*, April 1990

Michael Porter, *Competitive Strategy: Techniques for Analysing Industries and Competitors*, New York Free Press, 1980

Anne H. Reilly, 'Are Organizations Ready for a Crisis? A Managerial Scorecard', *Columbia Journal of World Business*, Vol.22, No. 1, Spring 1987, pp.79-88

Philip S. Scherer, 'The Turnaround Consultant Steers Corporate Renewal', *Journal of Management Consulting*, c. 1988

Edward M. Schulman, 'Two Methods for a Quick Cash Flow Analysis', *The Journal of Commercial Bank Lending*, June 1988

S. Slatter, *Corporate Recovery*, Penguin, 1984

T. Smith, *Accounting for Growth*, 1992

Mark Stevens, 'Turning Around a Troubled Company', *D&B Reports Journal*, Vol. 36, No.6, Nov/Dec 1988, pp 50-51

S.A. Tucker, *Profit Planning Decisions with Break-even Systems*, Gower, 1980

Lawrence R. Werner, 'When Crisis Strikes use a Message Action Plan', *Public Relations Journal*, Vol.46, No.8, 1990, Pp.30-31

Index

A

Abbots, Henry 166
ABC Ltd 100
acceptance credit facilities 149
accounts payable 25
accounts receivable 141
acquisitions 70
Acton, Cyril 58
added value 22
administrative expenses 75
advertising 11, 19, 22, 77, 125
AEC 31, 32
Aeon Group 153
age analysis 104
agricultural industry 23, 24, 118
Albion 31
aluminium 20, 22, 31, 164, 168, 169, 170, 171
Amanah Merchant Bank 192
amortization 177, 179
amortizing term loan 147
Amstrad 12
analysis of collections 118
application of funds 1
appraisal methods 100
Armitage Report on Lorries, People and the Environment 58
Ashley, Nicholas 156
Ashley, Sir Bernard 152, 155, 156
asset management 85
Aston Martin 23
Atkinson Lorries 39
Australia 38, 192
average
    annual net cash inflow 97
    rate of return 96

B

backstop facility 148
balance sheet 1, 141, 144
Ball, David 109, 115, 116, 117
balloon repayment 147
Banham, Russ 84

Bank of Canada 163
bank overdraft 72, 112, 139
bankruptcy 18, 140
bargaining power
    of buyers 11
    of suppliers 11
Barr plc 91
    net cash inflow 92
    cash flow statement 92
Beeching Report 38
Bibler, R S 67
bidding facilities 148
bills of exchange 149
Birmingham Motor Show 58
Black and Decker 12
Black, Lyn 120, 121, 122, 131
Blower & Co 117
Bloy Ltd. 165
BMW 190
Boalloy 34
Bognor Regis 184
Bollinger 23
bond with equity warrants 151
Boyadjian & Warren 27
brand image 12, 18, 19
breakeven analysis chart 89-90
breakeven profile 89
British Road Services 33
Broadbent, Gerald 34, 37
Brussels Motor Show 39
bullet repayment 147
business
    cycle 25, 26, 84
    demographics 137
    risk 84
Business Sector Classification 14
Business Times 189
Butts, Charlie 35
Buxton 35

C

Calgary 115, 163
Calgary Commercial Bank 163

Index

CAMPARI 127
Canada 115, 169, 174
Canada Aluminium Marketing Company Ltd (CAMCO) 168-169
Canada Bank Limited 159, 160, 163
Canada Basic Industries Corp. (CABIC) 165
Canada Monetary Agency 165
Canada National Oil Company 168
Canada Public Investment Fund (CPIF) 164
Canada Shareholding Company 164
Canadian Aluminium Company 158 - 183
    accounts receivable 180
    accruals 180
    acknowledgement 174
    advance payments 172
    assignment 174
    Board of Directors 166
    capital commitments 183
    capital reserve 181
    deferred charges 179
    facilities 166, 167
    financial charges 183
    financial performance 170
    information memorandum 159
    lenders' security 174
    Line 4 Equity 180
    memorandum 160
    notes to the 1993 Final 177
    off-take arrangements 168
    prepayments 180
    product mix 167
    provisions 182
    qualifying debt 172
    risk alleviating factors 170
    risks 170
    security arrangements 171
    Security Trust Deed 173, 174
    share capital 180
    shareholders 180
    statement of cash flow 176
    Statement of Income 175
    statutory reserve 181
    supply 168
Canadian Government 162, 163, 164, 167, 168, 171, 172
CAPEX 4
capital appraisal 100
capital cycle 7
    diagram 5, 6, 72-73
capital employed 114
capital expenditure 75, 76, 96, 100
    appraisal methods 100
capital investment 11, 96, 100
capital market activity 137
Cartier 23

Cartwright, Sid 36
cash 17
    conversion 85
    conversion cycle 84- 86
    crisis 139
cash flow 7, 12, 17-18, 22-23, 29, 34, 61, 72, 74-77, 84, 88-89, 91, 94, 96, 106-108, 117-118, 122, 128-129, 136, 138, 140-141, 144, 158, 176, 185, 193
    and business cycles 5
    capital expenditure decisions 98
    cycle 94
    dynamics 14
    forecast 118, 129, 144
    free 70-71
    generated 5
    management 30
    planning 128
    requirements 72
    statement 1, 2, 158, 195
    Volatility of 89
    Worksheet 118
cash flows 16, 19, 24, 66, 70-71, 88, 91, 97, 100, 193
    managing 72
    pattern of 77
cash generation 3, 88
cash inflow 100
    and outflows 100
Cash is King 5
cash outlay 31
cash reserves 89
Cash Tank diagram 87-88
Caswell, Danny 85
Caterpillar Construction Equipment 12
Central Planning Commission 165
Chanel 23, 155
China 186
Citibank NA 163
Citicorp 151
Clayton Dewandre 31
Cleckheaton 115
Commercial Companies Law 181
Commercial Motor 37, 38, 39, 59
commercial paper (CP) 145, 147-148, 151
commodity 22, 24
    traders 26
company liquidity 40
competitive
    advantage 17
    position 7
    trends 7
components 31
conglomerates 14, 15
Consolidated Plantations 185, 186

Construction and Use Regulations,
    1964 38
    1972 39
consumer recognition 19
convertible bond 151
corporate objectives 9
corporate specialist 108
corporates 146
cost classification exercise 89
CP (Common Parts) Series 59
CPIF 165, 166, 168, 171
creative businesses 23
credit 118
    availability 137
    controllers 76
    rating 74
    -risk appraisal 72
creditor 112
    analysis 104, 105, 134
    balance 112
creditors 3, 26, 72, 100, 104, 107, 112, 113-114, 116, 117, 118, 124, 126, 132, 134, 136, 141, 171, 194
creditworthiness 74
Cricklade Creameries 36
Cummins 35, 38, 39, 40, 59
current
    assets 41, 114
    liabilities 41, 72, 114
    liability 72
    trends 7
customer
    covenant 76
    loyalty 12
    service. 142
cyclical manufacturing industries 26

D

Daf 58
Daily Telegraph 153
Datuk Khatijah Ahmad 190
David Brown 31, 35, 36, 40
debenture figures 130
debt 5, 15, 72, 88, 89, 94
    restructuring 136
    servicing costs 89
    structuring 144, 157
    to equity ratio 61
debtor(s) 3, 25, 26, 76, 100, 102, 104, 107, 112, 113, 114, 116, 124, 126, 132, 133, 134, 194
    analysis 103
    control 102
    spread 102

decline,
    early 138
    late 139
    mid-term 139
decline phase 19
decoration 74
deferred tax 4
Dell Computer Corp. 84-86
    Snapshot 86
demand variability 26
demerging businesses 15
depreciation 96, 177
developing
    markets 23
    products 23
differentiation 12
Dimensions trailer 118, 121, 133
Discounted Cash Flow Technique 66-68, 99
discounted inflows 97
discounting 97
discretionary expenses 75
disposals 70
distinctive product features 18
distribution 18, 19, 23, 77
diversification 15
dividends 3, 4, 7
Double L 113, 115
downsizing 76
drawdown 161
drugs industry 16-17

E

E R Foden and Son Diesel (ERF) 30-71
    54GSF 35
    5LW 33, 36
    6LX 35
    88.R 37
    1982 Accounts 42, 45, 57
    1995 Consolidated Balance Sheet 62
    1995 Consolidated Cash Flow Statement 63
    A-Series 39
    B-Series 39, 40
    book values 71
    C-Series cab 59
    C36 Trailblazer 58
    cash flow data 70
    CFE 43
    CI4 31, 32, 33
    CI5 33
    commercial vehicle operations 42
    Consolidated Balance Sheet 1982 48
    Consolidated Profit and Loss Account 1982 47
    diesel lorry 31

dividend proposals 1982 42
E-Series 40, 59
E10 36
ES6 37, 59
Fire Engineering division 40, 58
Group Results for last ten years 60
historic cash flows 66
KV cab 34-35, 37
LK44 33
LV 37, 39
M-Series 40
M16 59
OE3 33
other group activities 1982 43
Plastics 43
Results, 1982 46
Share Option Schemes 64
SMC panels 40
South African subsidiary 42
SP (steel/plastic) cab 40
Statement of Source and Application of Funds 49
Streamline cab 33
Valuation 1995 64
Weightsaver 58
early warning signals 137
earnings from investments 3
Eaton 33, 59
economic
    boom 25
    cycles 30
    recession 25
economies of scale 11, 18
Egan, Victoria 156, 157
Elworth 31
employees 141, 143
Enasa 39
enforcement event 173
equity 5, 15, 17, 65, 82, 84, 121, 149
    markets 15
Ernst & Young 164
establishment expenses 74
eurobonds 146
eurodollar financing 145
European Coal and Steel Community 58
Eurotruck 39
Evening Standard 154
evergreen
    facility 150
    loan 150
ex-growth 18
express strategy 7
Extel Financial Ltd 152

F

factoring 102
Fallon, Peter 37
Faulkner, George 31
Ferrari 23
financial
    control 18
    institutions 146
    ratios 142
    Reporting Standard (FRS) No. 1 1, 5, 61
Financial Times 14, 152, 154, 155, 156, 157, 184, 187, 188
fixed
    assets 7, 19, 76, 88, 102, 114
    bond issues 150
floating rate notes 151
Fodens 30, 31, 32, 39, 58
Foden, Dennis 30, 34, 37
Foden, Edwin Richard 30, 34
Foden, Peter 34, 35, 37, 46, 58, 59
food industry 24, 26, 84
fragmented markets 23
France 33
Frank Hawkins Kenan Institute of Private Enterprise 136
full stock analysis 135
Fuller 38, 40, 58
funding movement 88

G

Gardner 31-36, 38-40
gearing 96, 152
geographical advantages 18
GKN 78, 79, 81
    1983 Annual Report and Accounts 82
Glaxo 150
global suppliers 18
grace period 4
Green, Eric 44
grocery retailers 26
Gucci 155

H

Hall's Toffee 32
Haslehurst, Geoff 154
Hastings Deering 190
Higginson, Andrew 153
high gearing 94
highly leveraged transactions (HLTs) 149
Hilary House 31
Hino 59
Hoare, David 155, 156

Hong Kong 150, 186, 189, 190, 191, 192
HR Trailers Ltd (HRT) 118-135
    Accountant's Report 133
    Cash flow Forecast 127
    Consolidated Balance Sheet 124
    Financial Position 122
    Financial Report 122
    Forecast Balance Sheet 126
    Forecast Profit and Loss Account 125
    management 120
    Management Accounts 132
    margin 128
    Summarized Profit and Loss Account 124
Hunt, George 36

I

ICI 35
implied strategy 7
Independent, The 153
Indonesia 189
industry economics 9
    identification 9
infrastructure 15
    projects 144
initial cash outlay 97
input price variability 26
insurance companies 30
Intel 17
intellectual property 18
interbank market 145
interest 4, 42, 74, 84, 88, 94, 97
    and dividends paid 3
    received 3
internal rate of return 97
International Accounting Standard (IAS) No. 7 1
International Harvester 39
international trade 22
inventory 82, 85, 139-140, 177, 179, 194
investing activities 4
investment 96
Investment Research of Cambridge 154
Iowa Development Credit Corporation 115
Iveco Fords 37, 64
Iverson, Ann 154, 155

J

Japan 19, 152, 153, 156
Jennings 31, 34, 37
Jusco 152, 156

K

Kanter, Hermin 166

key
    risks 7
    success factor 30
Kirkstall 31
Klear View 34
Kuala Lumpur 185, 190
KUB Malaysia Bhd 192

L

labour costs 25, 74
    productivity 75
Laura Ashley 152-157
Law Debenture Trust Corporation (Cayman) Limited 171
Law of the Public Investments Fund 164
leasing 151
Lec Refrigeration 184, 186
Lendal Holdings Ltd 106-117
    Asset Valuations 116
    Audited Accounts 117
    Audited Consolidated Balance Sheet 109
    Balance Sheet 112
    Cash Flow Forecast 117
    Consolidated Balance Sheet 110
    Corporate Specialist Report 108
    Management Balance Sheet 111, 113
    Product Range 108
    Profit and Loss figures 117
    Profit & Loss Accounts 113
    Retained Earnings 112
    Schedule of Fixed Assets 111
Lendal Agricultural (Canadian) Limited 115
Lendal Holdings USA Ltd 114
leveraged buy-outs (LBOs) 149
Leyland 31
LIBOR (London InterBank Offered Rate) 145, 147, 160
life cycle 19, 29
liquidation 117, 140
liquidity 41, 75, 84-85, 100, 117, 118, 135, 145
LME 164
loan
    covenants 94
    syndication 157
Lockheed 31
long term
    investment decisions 84
    debt 84
longer payables 85
low
    cost base 18
    return on capital employed 9
lower cash outflow 100

Index

M

mail order 19
Malaya 185
Malaysia 169, 184, 185, 186, 188, 189, 192
Malaysian United Industries 156
Manchester Co-op 36
manufacturing process 75
    stock, analysis of 104
margin 77, 100, 128
    generation 75
    of safety 29
market
    share 17-19
    value of equity to book value of debt 142
    -led approach 16
marketing 18, 19, 29, 75, 77, 137, 138, 168
Mason, Sharon 166
Matador 32
material costs 125
mature
    industries 136
    markets 24
Maxmin, James 152, 153, 154
McCarthy Information Ltd 152, 153, 154
measures of economic growth 137
medium-term notes (MTNs) 146, 151
Mega trailer 131, 133
Memorandum of Understanding (on aluminium) 168
Mercedes 12, 64
Meredith, Tom 84
mezzanine finance facilities 149-150
MGM 38
microprocessor chip market 17
Middlewich 39, 40
Milk Marketing Board 36
Milk Marque 36
Ministry of
    Supply 32
    Transport 38
Mitsubishi 190
multi option facility (MOF) 149
money market activity 137
monitoring 100, 101
Moreau, Pierre 115
Morris Commercials 36
Motor Show 31, 37, 38, 39, 59
multi currency loan 148

N

National Bank of Canada 164
National Freight Consortium 33
Naylor, Ron 113, 115

negative
    cash flows 16-17
    entry point 42
    operating cash flow 26
net
    capex 4
    cash inflow 3-5
        before financing 5
    current asset movement position 102
    current assets 114
    present value 97
    working asset financing 82
    working assets 77, 79
new products 19
New York 150
New Zealand 38
NIC 105
Nicols (Vimto) Plc - Consolidated cash flow statement 91, 93
note issuance facility (NIF) 149
Nik Mohamed Nik Yaacob 185-186, 188-189
non-cash
    investment 76
    items 4
non-essential
    machinery 76
    maintenance 74
Normandy landings 33
Northampton 35
Norwest Bank 115
NWA Survey Data 84

O

Okada, Motoya 156
Okada, Takuya 152, 156
Old, Nick 120, 121, 122, 128
Olympia 31
operating
    activities 3
    cash flow 84
    leverage 29
    process 25
order book 121
overall cost leadership 12
overdraft 118, 123, 131
overheads 25, 74, 112

P

P/E ratio 15
Paccar 58
paper 9
    making 24
patent 17
    rights 18
payback 96

PAYE 105, 113
payroll 139
perfumes 23
Permanent NWA 82
petrol stations 19
Philippines 186, 190, 192
pig industry 107
Pitcher, M A 98
Porsche Cars 12
Porter's Five Forces Model 9-11
preferential
    creditors 105
    trade 104
price level changes 137
private placement 150
proceeds of sale of fixed assets 4
product
    development 30
    proliferation 19
production costs 74
profit 61, 138
    and loss account 1, 3, 4, 144
    centres 16
    decrease 138
    or loss on the sale of fixed assets 4
profitability 85, 100, 143, 144
    index 97
Project QM 58
promissory note 148
purchasing 75

Q

Quota Agreement 162
    1990 171, 172, 174
    1991 170

R

Ralph Lauren 155
RASC 33
rates of return on capital employed 9
raw materials 74, 75, 77, 104
re-engineering 17, 84
re-pricing strategy 142
receivables 194
receiverships, UK 95
recession 40, 43, 61, 79, 94, 123
redundancies 74
regulatory
    breakthrough 25
    requirements 25
Reliance Tankers 32
relocation 76
Renaults 37
reserves balance 112
retained earnings 112
retained earnings to total assets 142

return
    earned on the capital employed 97
    on capital invested 96
    on invested capital 85
    on investments 3
Revman 154
revolver 147
revolving credit 147-148
Rhyl 36
ringgit 188, 190
Robins, Gert 166
Rockwell 59
Rolls Royce 35, 37, 40
Romalpa 116, 134
    clause 133
    terms 103
Royal Army Service Corps 32
Royal Electrical and Mechanical Engineers 34
revolving underwriting facility (RUF) 149
running expenses 96

S

Sabrina 35
Sainsbury's 78, 79, 80
sale and leaseback 76
sales 82, 113, 125
    price variability 26
    prices 29, 77
    to total assets 142
Sandbach 32, 34, 38, 39, 58, 59
Saunders, K A 165
Scania 64
Scottish Motor Show 58
Scottish Trailers 121, 122, 124, 128, 129, 130
seasonal sales 82
sector risk 16
Security State Bank of Iowa 113, 115
security trustee 173
Seddon Atkinson 39
selling expenses 75
sensitivity analysis 144
servicing of finance 3
shake-out phase 18
share price 15
shareholders 25, 41, 82, 118, 122, 136, 143, 180, 188
Shaw, Jack 165, 166
Shell BP 37
Sherratt, Ernest 31, 32, 33, 34, 35, 38, 44
short-term
    bank overdraft 82
    markets 147
    paper 149

Index

shorter receivables 85
sick companies 136
sickness 15
significant accounting policies 177
Sime Bank Bhd 188, 189, 190, 191, 192, 193
Sime Darby 184-195
    cash flow statement 195
    Director's Review of Results 191
    Group Results 186, 192
    Interim Results 190
    Net cash inflow 194
Sime Darby Financial Services Holdings Sdn Bhd 192
SimeSecurities Bhd 188-189, 191
Simplon, Edward 165
Simplon Investments Limited (SI) 164, 165, 166, 168, 171
Singapore 190, 192
Smith Berry, Martin 190
Smith, Isaac 166
Smith, Raymond 166
source and application of funds 41
sovereigns 146
Spicer 58
sports shoe industry 11
stages of the cycle 16
stalemate markets 23-24
Standard Chartered Bank 164
standby
    facility 147
    loan 149
Star, The 192, 193
Statement of Changes in Financial Position 1
Statement of Source 1
steel 9, 26
Steyr 59
stock 75-76, 79, 100, 103-104, 111, 116-117, 126, 132, 179
Stock Exchange 190
Stock Market 122
stockholder 20
stocks 3, 97
stocktaking 76, 103
strategic cash management 30
Sun Micosystems Inc. 84
Sun Trailers 133
Sun Trailers (Far East) Inc 118, 123
Sun UK Ltd 120, 121, 122, 123, 127, 130, 131, 132, 134, 135
Sunderland 120
supplier rationalization 18
supply contracts 77
survival plan 117
sustainable growth rate 27-28
swingline facility 148

SWOT analysis 9
Sydney 193
syndicated loan 145, 147, 148, 150, 158
    features 146
synergy 14
synthetics 146

T

takeover 18
Tan Sri Nik Mohd Yaacob 193
Tautliner 34
tax 42
taxation 4, 7, 96, 162, 186, 191
technological
    breakthrough 25
    problems 25
telephone 76
    shopping 19
term loan 147
terms of trade 77
Texas 84, 86
Thailand 189
Thorneycroft 31
Thornton, John 155, 156
Times, The 153, 156
Tofte, Gudvin K 165
Toles, Alan 115
Tractors Malaysia 188
trade
    creditors 79
    debtors 79
trading loss 42
Traffic Act 30
transferable loan certificates 148
transferable loan
    facility 148
    instruments 148
turnaround 141, 142, 143, 144
    consultant 138, 140, 142, 143, 144, 151, 157
    manager 151
    methodologies 151, 157
    plan 140, 143, 144
    stategies 144
    strategy 143
    team 143
turning sales into cash 85
turnover 79, 112

U

UK 38, 39, 42, 44, 76, 84, 150
ultra-exotic technologies 23
unemployment 15
unit sales 77
United Malaysian Banking Corp. 185

United States 38, 84
University of North Carolina 136
US Caterpillar 185
USA 145, 150, 152

V

value
    added 21, 25, 26
    value chain 20, 22, 29
    chain analysis 22
variables 26
VAT 105, 124, 126
Vimto 91
volume
    manufacturing facilities 17
    markets 23, 24
    producers 18
Volvo 64

W

Walsh, Jim 155
washing powder business 19
Webb, Hugh Blakeway 154
Wedgewood 23
Wellcome Group 150
Western Australia 168
Western Star Trucks 64, 65, 71
    offer evaluation 65
wheel of competitive strategy 8, 9
Wheway, Albert 44
wood and metal fabrication 23
work in progress 76, 100, 103-104, 111-112, 116, 132
work-in-process 179
working
    capital 19, 72, 75, 100, 118
    capital behaviour 77
    capital cycle 31, 76, 88
    capital to total assets 142
    investment 77, 79
World War I 30
World War II 32, 33
Wrexham 40, 58

Y

Yahaya, Tunku Ahmad 185

About the author

Keith Checkley FCIB worked for many years at Barclays Bank where he held several management assignments in agricultural and corporate lending. He then assumed a senior position in the bank's credit and risk management team and was responsible for sector risk analysis, bank exposure monitoring and corporate restructuring.

More recently he has worked as a business consultant, designing programmes for many banks, corporates and financial institutions. He has had extensive experience lecturing and training in the UK, North America, Africa, the Caribbean, Eastern Europe and the Far East. Keith specialises in credit analysis, corporate recovery, corporate strategy and risk management.

Keith is an Associate Director of prebon training services where he designs and delivers dynamic, tailor-made training programmes that focus on the current issues surrounding the management of cash, credit analysis and strategy for both the corporate and banking sectors. Prebon Training Services specialise in delivering practical solutions to a broad range of training needs in both mature and developing financial and commodity markets and recently won the prestigious National Training Award.

A Fellow of the Chartered Institute of Bankers Keith is also a member of their National Speakers Panel. He has written ten books on business topics including *Finance for Framing, Finance for Small Businesses, Finance for Business, Advanced Credit Analysis, Lending* – a set study text from the CIB's ACIB/Degree qualification – and *Cash is King*.